KU-308-528

LIVERPOOL JMU LIBRARY

3 1111 01505 6342

GOLD *from the* STONE

Also by Lemn Sissay

Perceptions of the Pen
Tender Fingers in a Clenched Fist
Rebel Without Applause
Morning Breaks in the Elevator
The Fire People (ed.)
The Emperor's Watchmaker
Listener
Refugee Boy (play adaptation)

GOLD *from the* STONE

LEMN SISSAY

CANONGATE
Edinburgh · London

Published in Great Britain in 2016 by Canongate Books Ltd,
14 High Street, Edinburgh EH1 1TE

www.canongate.tv

2

Copyright © Lemn Sissay, 1985, 1988, 1992, 1999, 2008, 2016

The moral right of the author has been asserted

British Library Cataloguing-in-Publication Data
A catalogue record for this book is available on
request from the British Library

ISBN: 978 1 78211 909 8

Typeset in Sabon 9.25/12.25 pt by
Palimpsest Book Production Limited, Falkirk, Stirlingshire

Printed and bound in Great Britain by Clays Ltd, St Ives plc.

MIX
Paper from
responsible sources
FSC
www.fsc.org   FSC® C020471

To Dawn. Thanks for being there.

'How do you do it?' said night.
'How do you wake and shine?'
'I keep it simple,' said light.
'One day at a time.'

Contents

From REBEL WITHOUT APPLAUSE
(1992)

From MORNING BREAKS IN THE ELEVATOR
(1999)

From LISTENER
(2008)

NEW POEMS

INTRODUCTION

It's the 21st of May. Facebook and Twitter are overflowing with birthday wishes. I am sat in a café away from home, at the Bradford Literature Festival. My mother has sent me wishes from her apartment in New York. But that's the end of the story.

Family is a set of memories disputed between one group of people over a lifetime. Due to a near-lethal dose of racism delivered by The Institution I didn't know my mother until I was twenty-one. She approached social services to have me fostered for a short period of time while she studied. The social worker gave me to foster parents and said, 'Treat this as an adoption. He's yours forever. His name is Norman.' The foster parents gave up their experiment after twelve years and put me into a children's home and vowed never to contact me. I thought my name was Norman Greenwood.

I thought the world constantly smiled. I didn't realise that it was me smiling at the world smiling back at me. I was a popular kid and did a good sideline in poems for all occasions. My first commission and public reading was at the assembly hall at Leigh C of E, where I performed a poem to celebrate our year group on its last day. I still get Facebook messages about it from ex-pupils. But The Institution was determined to wipe the smile from my face.

At eighteen, the legal age of adulthood in England, I was officially uncoupled from The Institution and left to float into space. An administrative obligation was to give my birth certificate to a responsible adult – a parent or aunt or uncle. But I had none. They had to give the birth certificate to me. And there it was. My name, my true name, Lemn Sissay. And my mother's name, Yemarshet Sissay. From that moment onwards I took my name.

The only proof of my existence was in the poetry I had

written since the age of twelve. The social worker wanted to show that someone loved me and so he gave me a letter from my files. It was from my mother just a few months after I was born. She said, *'How can I get Lemn back? I want him to be with his own people in his own country. I don't want him to face discrimination.'* She was writing to a social worker whose name was Norman. He had named me after himself.

Family is a group of people proving each other's existence over a lifetime. Without family I had poems. In poetry I stuck a flag in the mountainside to mark where I had been. If a tree falls in the forest and nobody hears it then did it fall? So the saying goes. It did fall. And I know it because I wrote it down at the time. In poetry I sought documentary evidence that I existed at a given time. And, given time, I would investigate through the poems and find more evidence.

'Secrets are the stones that sink the boat.
Take them out. Look at them. Throw them out and float.'

My first professional reading was at seventeen. I was given night-release from Wood End – a prison for children. I read on stage at the Abasindi Coop, a black women's cooperative in the heart of Moss Side in Manchester. I was paid £25. It was 1983. I was rich for a night. I danced to reggae music and returned the next day to Wood End where I was strip-searched and placed back in regulation clothing.

With a birth certificate, a letter from my mother, and a fist full of poems I left the institution with two aims. The first was to find my family. The second was to become the poet whom I already was. Due to being moved from institution to institution I didn't know anyone who had known me for longer than a year. I was about to embark on a search for a family who didn't know me either.

In 1984, almost immediately after leaving Wood End, I approached a socialist printer called Stephen Hall of Eclipse Prints. I paid him on 'tic' (monthly) and printed 1,000 copies of *Perceptions of the Pen* which I sold to friends and the families of mill workers and striking miners. Poems from *Perceptions of the Pen* are in *The New British Poetry, 1968–88* edited by Gillian Allnutt and Fred D'Aguiar (Paladin Books).

Within a year I also set up my own business – A.S.W.A.D. Gutter Cleaning Services. I wrote a poem and printed it on a leaflet to drum up work. I posted it through the letterboxes of every house in my town. In 1986 I took my first play through a full run at the Edinburgh Fringe, at South Bridge Centre on Infirmary Street, with Pit Prop Theatre and Leigh Drama Centre. I had poems published in the local paper, *The Leigh Reporter*.

'I am not defined by my scars but by the incredible ability to heal.'

When my ladders were stolen the gutter-cleaning business was done, and so I moved from the Lilliputian villages of Lancashire to the great city, the OZ on the horizon – Manchester.

'Child says to me in a workshop, "Are you famous?"
I says, "The answer's in the question."'

What spurned my career then is the same as now – word of mouth. I started reading in community centres and theatres around the country. Word of Mouth. In 1987, when I was twenty, my poetry was accepted by *Bogle L'Ouverture Publications* in London. They were the first to publish Linton Kwesi Johnson in *Voices of The Living Dead* (1974) and Walter Rodney's *How Europe Underdeveloped Africa* (1972). The publishers, Jessica and Eric Huntley, cared for me as parents would a rebellious child about to go off to university. *Tender Fingers in a Clenched Fist* was published and a certain kind of national recognition ensued.

'Integrate is not a Northern Compliment: "'n't 'e great."'

Among others, the Caribbean poets in England laid the ground for me. Benjamin published his *Pen Rhythm* chapbook in 1980. Linton Kwesi Johnson, Benjamin Zephaniah, John Agard, Jean 'Binta' Breeze, Grace Nichols, Valerie Bloom, James Berry, and more. Linton has always been a royal presence as a man and reggae artist. Benjamin has always been the mature prince. Jean 'Binta' Breeze, the queen. I read with them throughout the country. They introduced me. They created space for me. In turn I brought many of them to Manchester.

In the 1980s most black poets had Caribbean accents. It would be some twenty years before second-generation African voices came through. I knew it then. The main Black British voices in poetry were Jackie Kay, Maud Sulter, Patience Agbabi, and myself. Is it a coincidence that three of them were either adopted or fostered and two of them were mixed race?

"'I'm a poet."
"But what does a poet do?" said the airhostess.
Saying "write" seemed churlish. "I do readings around
the world," I said.
She looked down at her palms.
"Will you read mine?" she said.'

In 1988, on publication of *Tender Fingers*, the *Guardian* ran a double-page article by Kate Muir: 'Lemn Sissay has success written all over his forehead.' But 'success' was a spark in a match factory. I was relative to no one. What was success if I had no one to prove myself for or against?

Any 'success written on my forehead' would only compound the unfathomable depths of loss. I could not release myself from this conundrum. I wanted to. I realised I would have to wait years for my friends to understand the importance of what they naturally took for granted. I would have to wait for them to have children, or for them to lose someone, before they felt a morsel of what I did. Thankfully some of them remember me saying as much.

'"Famous poet" is an oxymoron.'

To fulfill the role of 'family' I needed to prove what had happened to me in my first eighteen years, as there was no one else who could. I needed to find my family. I was performing around Britain and out across the world, writing commission, giving workshops, working in radio and all the stuff a young alive poet does. At each stage of my journey, and with each 'success' my sense of loss deepened.

'Have we been waiting to be accepted for so long that not being accepted has become the criteria for our acceptance.'

I may as well call it what it was. Racism. All the hallmarks were there. My name was stolen. I was stolen from my parents. I was experimented on. When the experiment didn't work I was placed in a darker institution. I didn't meet a black person until I was nine. I didn't *know* a black person until I was seventeen. I was nicknamed 'Chalky White' as a teenager. I internalised this racism. I owned it. But everything in the sixteen years that preceded it was just a warm up. The day I said 'stop' was when the nightmare began. And I spoke about this in my readings and in my poems. I had to.

'A Dutch MC asked me how she should introduce me on stage. "Just say 'He loves what he does and he does what he loves'," I replied. She walked on stage and said, "Lemn Sheeshay he likes what he does and does what he likes."'

But racism was a sideline. I couldn't allow myself to be defined by how well I articulated what I didn't like. As seductive as this was I found myself in a situation where my own anger could be commodified in the arts and, instinctively, I knew my anger ran too deep to be accommodated and paid for. There is a deeper level to anger, I believed. One that couldn't be sold or bought.

'Anger is an expression in the search for love.'

I needed answers to bigger questions. Why was I in the children's homes? Why did the foster parents throw me away? Who was my family? Where was I from? Why was I not returned to my mother? Why was my name changed? Where are the eighteen years of records about my life? I knew I had been lied to for seventeen years. The proof was in my name. The letter from my mother was to a social worker who had illegally named me after himself – Norman. I found my mother at twenty-one, in 1988. *Tender Fingers* is dedicated to her.

'Life is not worth living if there is no one that you would die for.'

Poetry was closer to me than family. My poems are photographs. And with two books under my belt at twenty-one they felt a point of record. There was nothing else that could bridge the emotional and physical stories other than poetry. My poems are my family. Sometimes when I perform or publish them it is like I've released them to scrutiny. It irritates me that anyone would criticise them. They are not perfect. They never pretended to be. They're my family. They are at different stages of development. And that's okay.

In the early 1990s I moved to Bloodaxe Books. I needed to move from my beloved Bogle *L'Ouverture* and Bloodaxe accepted me in 1992. I was twenty-five. I'd been out of the institutions for seven years, published for four. Bloodaxe published my book *Rebel Without Applause*. It sold out. What they didn't tell me was that they had no intention of reprinting. It would be eight years before I published another book. There was no Jessica and Eric to talk to. And Bloodaxe wouldn't return my calls. I had no idea why.

'They separated from me and pointed their fingers at me and shouted, "Are you integrating or separating or what?"'

Regardless, I spent the next eight years writing and performing, making radio documentaries and writing plays. Occasionally I would contact Bloodaxe to ask when they would reprint. I was contracted to them. They did nothing. I continued searching for my family. In 1995, in a BBC documentary called *Internal Flight*, I found my father and brothers and sisters. I also confirmed the childhood abuse I had suffered whilst in the institutions. Slowly the jigsaw was coming together. *Time Out* reviewed the documentary: 'Will this man not do anything for publicity?' it read. No book release from my publishers. Not a whisper.

Crazy as it sounds, on some level I believed I deserved to be treated this way. It was like being quietly beaten up in the corner of a busy room, by the person who invited me to the party, whilst also being accused of gatecrashing. Make of this what you will. It happened and it must be said. Seventeen years later I received an apology of sorts from Neil Astley of Bloodaxe for it was he. The apology accompanied a request that I change some detail about him on my website. Something that had always bothered him:

'It's not difficult to be successful in poetry but as a successful poet it is.'

My books are flags in the mountainside. I have another flag in broadcasting, another in public art, another in performance, in plays, in television, in music. I am the first of my generation, of the contemporary poets, to make poetry as public art. Today in England it is normal, but it wasn't in 1992. I started landmark poetry with Hardy's Well, in Manchester. My central influence is Ian Hamilton Finlay. I released an album in Germany, *Disjam Phuturing Lemn Sissay.*

By the age of thirty-two I'd found and visited all my family. I had travelled the world to find them: Ethiopia, Senegal, America, Europe. I had travelled the world to perform too.

'It's not difficult to be funny in poetry on stage. Just set up a false idea of what poetry is and then ridicule it, set up a false idea of what an audience is and then ridicule them – they'll love it.'

A new generation of poets were emerging out of their teens. A few years passed. I met Jamie Byng when filming a poem in the Spiegeltent at Edinburgh International Book Festival in

1994. The title of the poem was 'Gold From The Stone'. Jamie became the CEO of Canongate Books where he founded an imprint, Payback Press. The second syllable in 'Rebel Without Applause' rhymes with swell. Reb*el*. Reb*el* without applause. In the same year Bloomsbury published my children's book *The Emperor's Watchmaker*. In 2000 my next book *Morning Breaks In The Elevator* was published by Canongate. It sold out. Both these books are in print to this day

'If you are searching for your family the search begins when you find them.'

I've my own journey and it is unique. My conversation has not been with the gatekeepers or the ivory towers. Why would you storm an ivory tower unless you wanted to build one yourself? There are gatekeepers though. They need you to want to go through their gate. The more you want to go through their gate the more real their gate becomes. Poetry belongs in the world. The world belongs in poetry. I have always thought that way. I have always been that way.

'I've never thought of the artist's career as up or down. I see our careers as orbits. Each orbit is unique.'

So we come to my last book *Listener*. It was published by Canongate in 2008. It has a killer cover by Rankin. But the book is a third too big. And for that I apologise. I've always wanted to apologise for it.

My Landmark poems are on walls across the world. My radio documentaries have meant sitting in the home of Gil Scott-Heron while he makes me mango juice, or interviewing The Last Poets on street corners in Harlem. From walking on stage at Paul McCartney's book launch at the Queens Theatre or giving a workshop to homeless surfers in Durban, South Africa, I have been blessed with living my entire life as a poet. A life based on word of mouth above all. The life of a poet, and yet it only feel like it's beginning now.

So here is *Gold From The Stone: New and Selected Poems*. I have been a poet since I was twelve years old. I knew it then. I know it now. My journey has been kicked and punched at different times, and to be honest I am aware that I've tried to sabotage it myself at times too.

The best poems are unseen and unheard by anyone other than the person who wrote them and the persons they were intended for. They are read at funerals or between lovers or between daughters and fathers. They are kept within the family. Writer, audience, performer, performance and applause. It is the perfect journey for a poem: beginning, middle and end. The closest to that is a reader and a book.

'The idea that poetry is a minority sport has never rung true with me. Ever.'

At the start of *Rebel Without Applause* is the quote: 'if you are the big tree I am the small axe.' It is a quote from 'Small Axe' by Bob Marley. I was a fan of Bob Marley before I knew I was Ethiopian. My father was a pilot for Ethiopian Airlines and co-piloted The Emperor, Haile Selassie. Although my father died in 1974 I still have a picture of him in which he has the exact same ring on his finger as Bob Marley had on his hand.

An Ethiopian man said, 'Do you know what your name means? It is an unusual name.' I told him that I didn't. 'It means *Why?*'. If you are not from Ethiopia please don't think Ethiopians give their children questions as names. It is an unusual name in any culture. I had no idea what it meant until I was thirty-two. How could I be anything other than a poet with a name like '*Why*'?

PERCEPTIONS OF THE PEN

Well 'I'

Well, I am a poet and it is my life.
I would slit my wrist with a pen not a knife.
Well, I am a poet from now until then.
My life is my paper, my knife is my pen.

Mother

Mother, what will I say to you?
Will I tell you about what I've been through?
Mother, will you criticise?
Mother, will you see it through my eyes?

Mother, what will you say to me?
It's through your eyes I'd like to see.
Mother, will you criticise?
Mother, will you see it through my eyes?

Mother, what will you say to me?
Mother, will you read my poetry?
Am I just what you want me to be?
Mother, will you see it through my eyes?

Mother, what will you say to me?
Am I just what you want me to be,
Or, Mother, will you criticise?
Mother, will you see it through my eyes?

Ain't No

Ain't no clothes to wear, no
Ain't nobody to know
Ain't nowhere to come, nowhere to go
Ain't no belongings that last
Ain't no reminder of no past
Ain't no reason to give
Ain't no reason to live
Ain't no love to take
Ain't no love to fake
Ain't no reason to cheat
Ain't no body to beat
Ain't no body to belong
Ain't no one heard this song
Ain't even got a tune
Ain't even got a bloom
Ain't no mother
Ain't no father
Ain't no sister
Ain't no brother
Ain't no light for my cigarette

Ain't no cigarette . . .

Scream

Don't take what I have because what I have is me.
Don't steal my mind because it's nearly free.
How can I stay unpolluted,
Live in this world and still keep my head?

The things that I'm seeing is mind-blowing insight,
And the war that I'm fighting is a mind-blowing fight.
And the love that I'm feeling is less than a drip in a stream.
And the feel that I'm feeling is scream . . .

So Near and yet So Near

There's a man who lives in a London apartment,
And he's really blowing his mind,
Says it's the fault of the government.
And he thinks he's going blind,
Because all he sees is darkness,
But he says it's all a lark, yes.

There's a beggar who lives on his weak, so weak, knees
And he says he's losing his head,
Claims it's the fault of the zombies,
And the people in power are the living dead.
Says he thinks he's going to die,
But he knows it's the living dead who lie.

There's a teacher who lives in a school,
And he says he's going wild.
He says he knows what they are doing,
And everybody is filed.
He says he's going to learn
What the children should know,
Says he's started to burn,
But he cannot melt the snow.

There's a policeman who lives in a cell,
Says his job's like living in hell.
Says he must be heaven sent,
'Cause he's the only one who knows it's bent.
Yes, he wishes he could fly
So he could leave and live in the sky.

There's the old man who sits on the shelf,
Says he's losing his wealth,
And he could really care about his health,
And he couldn't really care about his health,
Just wealth . . .

There's the young boy who sits on the fence,
Says sitting on the fence don't make no sense,
Says he's going to have a child by a wife,
Cut the fraction with a knife.
There's always enough, but no one will explore
The shadow behind the door,
So near and yet so far . . .

As Is Life

The kingfisher plummets into the river
And captures the winding fish.
As is life . . .
The birdwatcher slowly gropes the ground for his binoculars,
Not daring to move his eyes from what he sees.
It could be fear in his eyes, it could be compassion.
His hands begin to get agitated
And so does he.
His eyes cringe as he cautiously looks for his binoculars,
His head turns to his binoculars, and he slowly reaches for them.
And a rustle of wings, a shimmer in the silent air,
The kingfisher in full flight,
Sinks into the silence of the mere.
The birdwatcher cocks his head to the side in an angry but what
Could have been a mellow moment.
As is life . . .

TENDER FINGERS IN A CLENCHED FIST

LIVERPOOL JOHN MOORES UNIVERSITY
LEARNING SERVICES

African Metaphor

You can't sweep dust under the rug any more.
You can't keep hiding bodies under the boards of the floor.

You can't sanction the hearts of an African race.
You can't hide a man from his very own face.
You can never be a king if you elect yourself the crown.
You cannot perceive the suffering if you've never been down.

You're on the great white colonial ego trip,
But soon you will be penned into your own township.
Your tables of justice will be turned until they fall upon
    your knees.

Our cries of injustice will drown your pathetic pleas.

You can't remember the Sharpeville massacre.
Do you remember the exploitation of Namibia?
You can't remember Mangaliso Sobukwe.
Do you remember the name Azania?

You can't sweep dust under the rug any more.
You can't keep hiding bodies under the boards of the floor.

You can't hear the trickle of blood that will stick your lips
    together.
You can close the curtains but you can't hide the weather.
You cannot smell the smoke while it is twisting in the air.
You can't feel the fire though it is singeing your hair.

You can't arrest the soul of an African revolutionary.
You can't meter the reaction of a reactionary.
You cannot hold an African metaphor.

You can't sweep dust under the rug any more.
You can't keep hiding bodies under the boards of the floor.

Your graves . . . your graves are already being dug by the
     gardeners of my country.
Your coffins are cut to measure by my sisters of carpentry.
If you cannot feel the illness then you'll never find the cure,
And you'll never be prepared for the African metaphor.

When mother delved the kitchen knife into the heart of the
     white beast
She closed her eyes tightly in the ecstasy of release.

You will feel the flames of vengeance in the deep heat of
     the night,
And the stench of scorching flesh will make you wish you'd
     seen the light.
You will hear the warrior cry, bang fiercely on your door.
You will see the horrifying death-defying anger of the African
     metaphor.

You can't sweep dust under the rug any more.
You can't keep hiding bodies under the boards of the floor.

Listening

Listening, and we're listening
To the ones who scream,
Hidden by the pounding sounds of the traffic.

We're listening
To the Blackness in the dream,
Hidden by the screams of this nightmare.
And it's getting louder.
People, we're getting louder.
People, we're turning round,
Crumbling the buildings to the very ground.

And we're feeling
The unsteady feel,
The breaking of the seal of unconsciousness.
Listening.

And we're breaking the dawn,
For this morning there's a different sound.
Keeping our ears to the well-trodden ground,
We're angry with the pain we hear.
There's an insecure feel in the air.

Because we're listening,
Like wolves in the dark,
Eagles in the sky.
Driven like cattle,
Ears to the ground.

We can hear the water.
We need water.
We need to quench our thirst.
But we're listening first.

Cautious as cats,
Punished as dogs,
We can hear the water.

The priest chants.
The congregation turn their heads.
The politician rants.
The people turn their heads.
Muffled screams and whispers,
Pointing fingers,
While the silence crawls from the inner city towns
And holds them in the fist of suspense,
And holds them
                    waiting
                         waiting
                              waiting
For the gutters to run with blood
And the sweet taste of victory in the mouths of the
    downtrodden.
And if you don't keep listening
You'll be caught unawares.
We're listening.
We're listening.
We're listening.

Nursery Rhyme

Humpty Dumpty was pushed,
But propaganda played its part.
And Little Jack Horner was paranoid,
One word would lose his heart.
So he pulled out a plum instead
To save his self from winding up dead.
He knew all the king's horses and all the king's men
Would never put Humpty together again.

Some Quotes from Neatherton Man Found in Deepest England Somewhere between 1974 and 1980

All the same.
Wogs go home.
Chalky, living in a blackboard.
Golly, it's a jam.
Toby, your name is Toby.
Monkey, lamppost swinger,
Hair like a sponge.

For breakfast
A bowl of coonflakes.
For tea
Coon on the cob.

Wipe off the coondensation.
Paki.
You're all right, but the other niggers . . .
Wog. Stay at home.
Nigger, wog, nigger.
Stab a nigger.
Rubber lips.

Splatted noses.
You can't give a black eye
To a black bastard.
Jungle bunny, go home.
Black girls are prostitutes.

Pakis smell of shit.
Get a wash, Paki.
NF. Wogs go home.
BNP. Give them a whitewash.

All good cricketers,
All fast runners.
It's because they run through the jungle.
As thin as an Ethiopian,
Poor as a Cambodian.
Kunta.
Your name is Toby.

Pink tongues, bright pink.
They've got white hands.
Big Black ugly nigger feet.
Tell us the one about the sambo.
Haven't I seen you on a jam jar?
Light his hair, it won't hurt his head.
Throw stones at his hair, it won't hurt.

Wipe fingers on coon's face.
Does it come off?
It's stuck on.
They take our jobs,
They take our women,
Send them home.
Wogs, go home.
Coons, go home.

Negotiations

For the radical faction to change the constitution
They should take their allegations to the institution.
So we took our allegations with a big bag of patience
Before we even met we felt the pain of prejudgement.
So we set up a meeting and gave the standard greeting
And if vibes could harm us we'd have got a good beating.
But the minutes were restricted and the picture they depicted
Was nothing but a smutter of the things we had presented.

But onward we went with constructive intention,
Keeping our strengths from personal friction.
But keeping the prevention of personal pretension
Was keeping construction in total detention,
Resulting in destruction and bad vibrations.

And a cut in the bag that was holding the patience,
And a cut in the bag that was holding the patience,
And a cut in the bag that was holding the patience.

Englabetween

Between the empty cans and dustbin lids,
Between the eyes of cats and tramps,
Incubated drunks mumbling incomprehensible bids,
Crashed out under yellow water lamps.
This is England, I said, on a soap box in the street.

What Have We Got

We've got a mountain on the horizon,
A sun on the floor,
The sea in the sky,
And the devil behind the door.

We've got a desert in a lake,
Islands in the city.
We've got the moon which is a fake,
And a bomb which is a pity.

We've got the stars when it's light,
Silence when it's not.
We've got friends, but they fight,
And what have we got?

We've got brother in the sky,
Sister in the sun.
Everybody's getting high
Yet no one's having fun.

We've got the rainfall,
We've got the snow.
Our sisters and brothers we call
And what do we know?

We've got a mountain on the horizon,
A sun on the floor,
The sea in the sky,
And the devil behind the door.

Moods of Rain

Rain twisting down the air poles
Like a broken river.
Slicing through the air. Cold
Biting me, I shiver.
Get your *Manchester Evening News*.
Soggy paper, running print,
I've got those winter dark blues.
Wet, cold, and skint.

The rip in the side of my pocket
Lets trickles of rain tickle the palm of my hand,
The picture distorted and wet in its locket.
Give me sunshine and sweet golden sand.

I'm giving up dodging glassy-eyed puddles,
My feet like the kitchen cloth,
Face screwed up, no time for scruples.
Head down, walk straight and cough,
And silver speckled my licks are crowned.
Melting Black faces drip and shine,
No smile but an unsatisfied frown,
Same goes, I think, for mine.

Stepping through mirrored streets,
Reflections of the dirty skies,
Soaked from my head to my feet,
Drips from my lashes sting in my eye.

It is raining, and I give way,
Soaking and cold I should smile.
What the hell I'm wet for today
And there's no use in getting so riled.

So kick the water, run down the road,
Hold your head up to the rain.

I was only feeling the cold,
Mind over matter over pain.

Soon I'll be home throwing off my coat,
Wrestling with my hair,
Warm and hungry for curried goat,
And the windows haze in the air.

My merry moods
Change like the weather.

Wasita

Was it a café window

or

A picture of a café window on a café wall

or

Was it a picture of a café wall and a café window on a café wall?

Sing a Song of Sick Penance

You and all your arrogance,
And all your golden rings,
Stating with your marriage,
To a tune that sings.

Sing a song of sixpence,
'Cause you have got more,
Jumped right over the fence
And landed on the poor.

You and all your grandeur,
And all your stately charm,
Got to a stately figure,
By bloodshed, death and harm.

Sing a song of sixpence,
'Cause you have got more,
Jumped right over the fence
And fell for ever more.

Sing a song of sixpence,
'Cause now you're sixpence less.
Jumped right over the fence
And now you're in a mess.

The Black Writers' Workshop

We are like cement, soft and protected,
Set hard and projected, the image

Of the mould of four hundred years,
We, the ever flowing
Tears of laughter and pain
Sprinkle our stories
Like light warm rain
On eyes that search for truth.
We, like cement, are weather proof.
We, the singers of dreams,
The echoes of screams,
The rivers of crying eyes,
Inject our words of truth, of love
Into the heart of life-living lies.

We are like cement, soft and protected,
To set hard and projected as the image.

Understanding Difference

I am the snake
That quietly flicked you that rosy red apple
When you was dying of thirst
In the sun-quenched desert,
The same snake you scuttled away from in hideous screams
of fear.

I am the lion's chest
That you lay your head on
When you were tired and had nowhere to sleep.
In the morning you lay still and petrified,
Only your darting eyes moved
Until I pounced away, pretending to be startled.

I am the nettle bush
That stung the beast, your enemy,
Until it lay groaning.
The same nettle bush you sliced with your machete.

I am the black person
That fights for equality,
Which is yours as well as mine . . .

The Day Will Come

The day will come
When the winners won,
The losers win.

The day will see
What the winners will be.
And the losers will be
Free . . .

The day will come
When the winners lose,
The losers choose.

The day will come
When the winners need
The losers . . . freed.

The Invasion of the Mancunoids

They've got shoulders straight as Hulme flyover,
Chins as square as the White Cliffs of Dover,
Pants as tight as a packet of Durex,
And thoughts as clear as beer fight sex.
Eye contact. A weird psychotic thing,
Because in their heads a bell does ring.

I'm a Mancunoid, fit and strong.
Your days are up and it won't be long.
If you look at me one second more
I'll beat your fuckin head in the fuckinwell floor.

Pint o' beer, Jon, what did you say?
It goes bloody well up every bloody day.
She's all right, what d'you think?
I bet I could have her if I buy her a drink.

Pint of beer, Jon, come on, pass it over here.
I think I'll give her a nudge, whoops, sorry, dear.
Have I got a job, have I got a car?
I've got lots of money and I'm going to go far.
Where do I live, what's my name?
I'm a macho Mancunoid man, I'll drive you insane.

I've got *don't mess with me* tattooed on my teeth,
I smile at old ladies and fill them with grief,
I've got a British Bulldog tattooed on my fist,
I wouldn't have done it but I was pretty well pissed.
But it's got a meaning . . . I'm part of the master race.
I'm from Manchester . . . and I'm ace.

I wear what's known as designer underwear
And socks at fifty pounds a pair.

I've got a bloodproof jumper just to stand the test.
I'm a manic mad macho Mancunian Manchester
    Mancunoid, so don't mess . . . with me.

And the other fifty.

The Red Death of Edgar Allan Poe

He held in his mind the fear
Of every human fool,
                    Clown
                    Or jack-in-a-box.

He rang the slow bell
                    Church chime
                    Death walk
                    No crime
                    Assassin
In his head so many times . . .

So many times he
Caressed the barbed wire of his own lines
That chilled his own skin
That bore his own death
Like he haunted himself
With his own breath.

He carved his name
Into mountains of depression
And he hastily drank river water
Where the dead sheep lay twitching.
Twitching in nervous song, he so often
Scaled the ornaments of his lonely
Mantelpiece.

Couldn't
Find
The
Coal
For the fire
Edgar Allan Poe
Couldn't

Find
The
Coal
For the fire . . .

Trying Me

Patience,
The dew drop dangling
On back-bending grass

Will fall to form
Tidal waves in ponds
Hidden in lonely fields.

Fingerprints
Embedded in a forehead
Are evidence.

Eyebrows
From slant to attention
You could walk across them.

Fingers
Tapping holes in a wooden table,
Splinters of truth bite my fingernail.

Landscapes,
Faces in the foreground,
Objectives in the back.

Spillage,
The tidal wave panic,
Frantically waving hands.

Decision
Tapping holes into the wooden table
Until it falls apart.

Truth
Washed by hand in the pond
By a tattily dressed woman.

Yearning,
An illness called truth,
Washed by a mourner.

Realism,
The pond shakes into a river
Terrorising my day-to-day life.

Enrapture
Consuming my thoughts
By the gulp.

Pulse,
The fingerprint
Matched the finger.

Blame
The constant falling
Of the dew drop.

Dead Wood Poetry

Gnarled tree of silence,
Why have you grown to rot today?
To avoid the beam of life, it seems.
You have grown to die today,
Gnarled tree of existence,
With eczema in place of your bark.
All your trinkets have fallen to the floor
And now you're left in the dark.

Fell Off and Fell Out

Connect cold ice with fire
And the ice melts to find
Broken telephone wire
Tangled in mangled minds.

We . . . we ran like the water,
Cupped in hands,
And splashed like the water
That splits lands.

Bad Trip – L.S.D.

The daisy that spits pure acid,
Burns pure consciousness.
Darkness becomes valid
So too does unhappiness.

Night creeps in with long spindle fingers
And scratches slowly in the mind.
White screams haunt from soul singers,
The rope begins to bind.

Slow tightening sounds,
White pointed masks, slits for eyes,
Splurging from the bubbling ground.
Fire spits from the skies.
Fire spits from the skies.

Melts your scarred and burning face.
You did the wrong thing.
Wrong time, wrong place.
Flower with a sting.
Flower with a sting.

Attracted by distortion,
Difference and change,
Too late for disillusion,
It has bound you in chains.

To drown you in the river,
Drown you in the sea,
Turned you on to make you shiver,
L.S.D.

Turned you on to make you shiver,
L.S.D.

Burn My Book (Burn In Illusion)

Don't bandage my words around the wrong bruises.
Don't sell yourself to the hoard of accusers.
Don't generalise what you can't bother to question.
Don't smash the mirror without seeing the reflection.

Don't burn my words in passive disbelief.
Don't disband your thoughts while turning overleaf.
Don't submit yourself to non-acceptance.
Don't surrender yourself to inno . . . ignorance.

Don't ask me to justify all that I write.
Don't ask me to tell you that you are all right.
Don't take offence when faced with the truth.
Just because they are sentiments presented by the youth.

Accept that my motivation brought me here.
Accept that there must be something to clear.
Don't close up and fall like a faulty telescope.
Blurred in your vision, void of question and hope.

And in all of this acknowledge, I don't only see the knocks,
Not just the pain, not just the shocks.
Where there is pain so too is love.
And the hand may well be soft and yielding
                              Wrapped in a velvet glove . . .

Tense Tattered Tortured Tried Tested and Torn

I am a tree with no roots . . . or dead roots . . . or
chemical-ridden roots.
I am an emotion with no colour. I am a colourless dream.
I am a scream.
I am a tear spiked with acid that runs burning down
tender cheeks.
I am the decisive decade, the moaning month, the harrowing
Hour, the stretched second, the weakest week,
I am the charred, twisted and broken branch of my grand
ancestral tree.
I am the burden of the recognition of something that never
happened to me.
I am the tragic trauma . . . tense, tattered, tortured, tried,
tested and torn.
I am still underdeveloped, without life, I am stillborn.
I am the stolen manuscript. The paper in the fire. The
unwritten anthology.
I am an ape, victimised by the poking of the iron rod of
anthropology.
I am the maroon nightmare. The muffled cries of a child
turning in his pillow.
I am yesterday and always tomorrow . . . always tomorrow
. . . tomorrow.
I am the epitome of the Western world's real dream.
I am the colourless dream. I am a scream.
I am the glued-together statue of a man.
I am the fickle face of one in a million.
I am the colourless dream. I am a scream.
I cry but then laugh and slowly smile.
I can only be a broken man for a short while.

Mother Thatcher

Whose is the gutter,
Mother Thatcher?

The one that swills away the poor,
Sucks them down the grid of non-acceptance,
The grid outside your door.
Man pride
In your prime,
Minister.
Whose is the gutter,
Maladminister?

Whose is the gutter,
Mother Thatcher?

What's that stagnant smell?
Oh, it's a miner problem, said she.
And nobody can tell.
Tell me a story, Mother Thatcher.
Jackanory, Jackanory.
If you're on high pay become a Tory,
Anything to uprise from.

Whose is the gutter,
Mother Thatcher?

Where the rats dare not go,
Where the breath smells bad,
Can't afford toothpaste.
And the water that runs is laced with
Toryism – Toryite.

VOTE FOR ME, it'll be all right.
But

Whose is the gutter,
Mother Thatcher?

Today Will Pass

Dew drops in the morning,
The fallen tears of the night,
Evaporate in the ever dawning of daylight.

And here comes the day after,
The sun climbs above the horizon.
Cries turn to relief and laughter,
And the metal melts from the prison.

When tomorrow leaves you
Then you will cry.
But tomorrow stays by you
While today slips by.

Look the other way to your fear,
Happiness needs no excuse.
Flick away a fallen tear,
Let go, get off and let loose.

When tomorrow leaves you
You're sure you will cry.
So you hold tomorrow with you
And today passed by.

Spell Bound

Spell bound,
New found,
I scaled
And unveiled
Racism.

Mass production,
Pure convulsion,
Bodily function,
Jerky revulsion,
Racism.

Took
A quick look.
It has changed
And deranged
Into terror.
Genetic,
Rhetoric,
Racism.

Spell bound,
New found,
I scaled
And unveiled
Racism.

Everything Is Rhythmical

Rhythm, rhythm,
Can you
Hear the
Rhythms?

Quick rhythm,
Slow rhythm,
God-given,
Life-living.

Rhythm, rhythm,
Can you
Hear the
Rhythms, rhythms?

If you listen close,
Ears to the ground,
The basis of noise
Is rhythm sound.
From spoken words to ways of walk,
From rappin' to reggae and funk we talk in.

Rhythm, rhythm
Can you
Hear the
Rhythms?

Way back in the heart of Africa,
They took our drums away,
But rhythm proved its own power
By being here today.
All four corners these sweet-sounding rhythms reach,
With treble in the speaker, even bass in the speech,

To the freezing cold and heat in heights,
Muhammad Ali did do it in his fights
With
Quick rhythm slick rhythm
bold rhythm gold rhythm
God given life living

Rhythm rhythm
Can you
hear the
Rhythm.

Sleep Is a Songbird

Sleep is a goddess to me now,
A whisper of continuous sentences
Bellowed in the daytime
Like a songbird in the night.

Tender is the pillow that soaks
My tears and wipes them from
My dreams. Consoling is the mattress
Like words of a lost mother.

I insert the needle of sleep
With a sigh of relief,
And hallucinate beauty from pain
And laughs from grief.

I sink like the tomb into the earth,
In wilful relief from all,
And lie cold yet warm,
Cushioned and calm.
Sleep is a songbird to me now.

Director's Notes (For the Daily
Shun and Daily Killer)

Bring on the dancing juries
And cat-caressing judges.
Bring on the soliciting solicitors
With empty veins and smelly crutches.

Enter the manic newscaster.
Exit the smoke.
Audition the junkie as a jester,
Give him an arm full of coke.

Q the lights for the New Cross massacre.
Fade the lights on the heartache and pain.
Leave a shadow for the exit of the murderer.
Then bring the lights up again.

Yes . . . Black skin looks menacing in white light!

She Read as She Cradled

You part of me.

Every day your history,
Every tomorrow your destiny,
Every growth your mystery,
Every mother wants a baby
                like you.

Every laugh your personality,
Every look your clarity,
Every word your stability,
Every mother wants a baby
                like you.

Every hiccup a comedy,
Every fall a catastrophe,
Every worry my worry,
Every step you're beside me,
Every sight you're pure beauty,
Every mother wants a baby
                like you.

Every tear wiped carefully,
Every word spoke lovingly,
Every meal fed silently,
Every cloth washed caringly,
Every song sung sweetly.

Every day I whisper quietly,
Every mother wants a baby
                like you.

City Sigh

Move
Quick
Slick
Time
Tick
Goodbye
On a
High.

City sigh,
Got to fly,
Don't know why.

Train
Plane
Sun
Rain
Fun
Pain
Be sane
Play the game
City rain
City pain
Here gone
Quick food
Pass on
Plastic too
Sit to brood
And look at you
Losing time
Meaning
Leaning
On the building
Of the

City sigh,
Got to fly,
Don't know why.

Burger food
Good to spew
To take away
Why not stay?
Instead you
People breathe
Bodies seethe
Babies teeth
And underneath
Is the

City sigh,
Got to fly,
Don't know why.

Live, man, die.

Spell Me Freedom

Spell me freedom
And make it simple,
So when I eat
It shall not make me sick.

Spell me freedom
And make the ingredients carefully,
So when I drink
It does not make me choke.

Spell me freedom
And whisper it quietly,
So when we speak
It does not give me a headache.

Spell me freedom
And bake it fresh,
So when I'm thirsty
It shall not make me dry.

Spell me freedom
And stir it quickly,
So when I taste
It shall not burn my tongue.

Spell me freedom
And tell the joke well,
So that when I laugh
It shall not unveil into hopeless tears.

Spell me freedom
And cradle each word,
That when I use them
They shall not crack like spines.

Interim and Cost

So who has lost,
Paid the cost?

Whatever is said,
Whatever is said.
Whatever is known,
Whatever is known.
Whatever is done,
Whatever is done.
Whatever is trust,
Whatever is trust.
Whatever is written,
Whatever is written.
Whatever is truth,
Whatever is truth.
Whatever is lost,
Whatever is lost.
Who has paid the cost?

Ace Under My Sleeve

British? Black and beautiful.
Check it out, my friend, we're radical.
And let us give
The will to live
To those who eat yet are not full.

The rose that grew up from the thorn,
The soil is good so throw the corn,
And let us feel
This fruit is real
For youth to eat from whence they're born.

Eradicate the ignorance
By positive deliverance,
So what we say
In any way
Is nothing but the truth enhanced.

Let us not cry to a crier
Nor look up when we are higher.
It's not hard
To play the card.
Come, let the truth confront the liar.

British? Black and beautiful.
Check it out, my friend, we're radical.
And let us give
The will to live
To those who eat yet are not full.

Traces

Dust spurts from the track
In the kick of a racing heel
And settles awaiting finale.
Smoke circles the lightbulb,
Painting the air a rich blue.
Shadows scamper past
Like the flick of a cigarette
To rest in the mirror lake.
Water gurgles down the plughole
Like a frightened mouse,
To disappear into echoing chatter.
The door shuts to the howling wind
In the wake of pressure.

Traces
Of what could have been,
Of what was.

The Show Goes On

The Arts Council criteria for funding is to conform,
So if they pay the revolution, the revolution will perform.

And if you can write along this dotted line your role in this
   society
Then you can play allegiance to the notorious great race
   robbery.
And with a knowing glint in their eye they'll say you can apply,
Then they'll stuff your open mouths with a piece of American
   pie

Saying . . .

The Arts Council criteria for funding is to conform,
And as we are paying the revolution, the revolution will
   perform.

And like puppets on barbed wire
We dance in this fire
And we – becoming the actresses and actors – are forgetting
   the plot.

Knowing so much that we needed something but not knowing
   what.
And we try to ignore this cynicism while stuffing our pockets
   with gold,
Saying, well, if they give it then take it, that's what I was told.

But the Arts Council criteria for funding is to conform,
Which means if they pay the revolution, the revolution will
   perform.

And Marcus Garvey turns in his grave seeing the liberalism
   he fought,
Seeing the modern-day slave being sold and being bought.

One slave was allocated to dance, another was commissioned
   to write poetry.
It was an unwritten law that if we dance, write, sing and paint,
                              we will forget about our slavery.

Time is being intricately fooled, and we are the fools,
'Cause if we take a look over the chimney pots we're being
   ridiculed.
Yes, the revolution will be hidden for another hundred years,
Or at least as long as governmental funding is here.
And an added bonus is getting us to believe in multiculturalism,
Again keeping our minds from the real situation.

That the Arts Council criteria for funding is to conform,
And if it pays the revolution, the revolution will perform.

Yes, we are a beautiful people, because through all this we
   still see light,
But just like the winter
The days are getting shorter,
And will we know what to do in the night?

Every second counts, every minute minute, every haunting hour.
This country is exerting a silent massacre.
Every second counts, every minute minute, every harrowing
   hour.
Ask yourself and seek the answer: where is the fund for
Black Power?

REBEL WITHOUT APPLAUSE

Bearing Witness

(Dedicated to James Baldwin who in his last recorded interview said black writers should bear witness to the times.)

Bearing witness to the times
Where it pays to sell lines,
Where African thighs thrive for twenty-five,
And guns run with the midnight son.

Bearing witness to the days
Of the blue-eyed glaze
In the black-eyed girl of the world
Whose life depends on a contact lens.

Bearing witness to the screams
Of children cut on shattered dreams,
Colonialised minds lost in times
Of permanent frowns and nervous breakdowns.

Bearing witness to the signs
Of white sandstorms in black minds,
Of waves from the west with white dagger crests
Scratching the black beaches back.

Bearing witness to the hour
Where maladjusted power
Realigns its crimes in token signs,
Then perversely repents with self-punishment.

Bearing witness to the times
Where black people define
The debt yet to be paid, you bet.
I'll be rhyming the fact when I witness that.

Remember How We Forgot

We don't cram around the radio any more.
We have arrived at the multi-dimensional war
Where diplomats chew it up and spew it up,
and we stand like orphans with empty cups.
'There will be no peace,' the press release
Said. 'The likelihood of war is on the increase.'
We are being soaked in a potion,
Massaged with a lotion, to calm the commotion
that hides the embers of the fire.
There's nothing as quick as a liar.
Don't you learn your lesson?
Are you so effervescent that
When they say day is day and it's dark in your window,
You say 'okay' and listen more tomorrow?
Seems you heard the trigger word.
You are space to be replaced, your dreams defaced.
Heavy questions quickly sink,
Leaving no trace – a spiked drink.
What kind of trip are you on?
Don't you remember the last one?
Remember how we forgot about Vietnam,
Afghanistan? Will you fall or stand
For a dream you haven't seen?
I'm afraid you will, you've taken the pill.
You're totally stoned on war.

Media hype and the slogans they write,
Is that all it takes to set you alight?
There's nothing better than a doped mind
For a young unemployed man to sign.
Figures go down when young men sign up.
What better when they're losing the votes, than to erupt
Into the uniting sound of war fever.
'We need unity now more than ever . . .
We shall only attack to righteously defend!'

Paranoia seeps in:
'Are you one of us or one of them?'
Slogans fall like hard rain as the government calls
For its children to break down the walls
of someone somewhere in some country
that is suddenly so vital to history.
Young men hang in their own fear . . .
But we don't cover that story, not here.
Not when we are in a battle that must be won.
Don't you understand there's a war going on?
More than ever we should pull together.
These are days of stormy weather
Where the patriots show their faces
And nationalists recruit places.
As the fear of the foreigner arises,
The race attack count rises,
Victims of the small island mentality.
England is no Mother country.
He holds the fear of The Awakening,
Of his shivering shores breaking
Like those in the Middle East did
When he raped it.
Will you take it, take this, without question,
fall in line with the press and the politician?
Remember how we forgot about Vietnam,
Afghanistan? Will you fall or stand
For a dream you haven't seen?
I'm afraid you will, you've taken the pill.
You're totally stoned on war.

Fingerprints

I can see your fingerprints
Fumbled all over this dead boy's body.
Can see them in his
Lifeless eyes,
In his fist clutched
By rigor mortis.
And holding up your hands to calm us people
You say: 'This was not a racial attack.'

I can see the wipe marks
On his forehead,
Where with the side of your fist
You tried to wipe them in

> Smudge them in
> Reshape them
> Rub them in
> Distort them
> Change them
> Hide them
> Rearrange them

> With ink that dried
> Before he died.

You report: 'We understand the victim was Black.
This was not a racial attack.'

Occupations

I don't need an occupation
To get picked up on the street.
I don't need an occupation
To be the victim of deceit.

I don't need an occupation
To get my pockets searched.
I don't need an occupation
To get kicked where it hurts.

I don't need an occupation
For basic rights to be taken away.
I don't need an occupation
To visit the cells for a day.

I don't need an occupation
To be living underneath.
I don't need an occupation
To feel a boot within my teeth.

I don't need an occupation
To be pestered constantly.
I don't need an occupation
To be hounded by the beast.

They are getting paid
When they're harassing me,
When they're writing out
False confessions of a robbery.

And in the cells I felt a rhyme
Riddle with a rhythm inside of me.
If the judgement fits the crime,
Get them when they're off duty.

Boiling Up

Can you spread me lightly on this street?
I would like to blend in.
If butter and bread can do it, so can I.

Will you sprinkle me softly in this hotel?
I would like to blend in.
If chicken and seasoning can do it, so can I.

(The store detective is either trying to
strike up some kind of meaningful relationship with me,
or I've got a box of jelly babies stuck to my left ear.)

Could you drip me into this club?
I would like to blend in.
If coffee and milk can do it, so can I.

(It's not a sawn-off shotgun in my inside pocket,
and that's not because I keep my machete there –
ten Regal King Size, please.)

Can you grate me into this city?
I would like to blend in.
If cheese and tomatoes can do it, so can I.

Can you soak me into this country?
I would like to blend in.
If rice and peas can do it, so can I.

Instant Consciousness

Instant consciousness comes in the pound,
Pay at the town hall and spread it around.
Love it or hate it, who are we to debate it?
We're so glad you've got it and daren't underrate it.

Because now you can serve us with the new vision,
Teach all us blacks about multiculturalism,
Then propose that if we don't listen to you
We're as bad as the rest, we're racist too.

It comes in a packet, doesn't cause no pain,
You buy it in toilets, no guilt and no shame.
The councillor says it's the product of the day,
There's money in it, and you don't have to pay.

It's taken us so long, you get there so fast,
Getting jobs to stop harassment while we get harassed.
Thanks for inviting me to dinner, I think I'm getting fat.
Instant Consciousness – I'd love some more of that.

Airmail to a Dictionary

Black is . . . the shawl of the night,
Secure from sharp paranoiac light.

Black is . . . the pupil of the eye,
Putting colour in the sea's skin and earthen sky.

Black is . . . the oil of the engine,
On which this whole world is depending.

Black is . . . light years of space,
Holding on its little finger this human race.

Black is . . . the colour of ink,
That makes the history books we print.

Black is . . . the army. Wars in the night,
Putting on the Black to hide the white.

Black is . . . the colour of coal,
Giving work to the miners, warmth to the old.

Black is . . . the shade of the tree,
Sharp in definition against inequality.

Black is . . . the eclipse of the sun,
Displaying its power to every one.

Black is . . . the ink from a history,
That shall redefine the dictionary.

Black on Black is Black is Black is,
Strong as asphalt and tarmac is.

Black is . . . a word that I love to see,
Black is that, yeah, black is me.

The Customs Men

Breaking out from the plane,
Home's mouth lays wide open
From the white oesophagus corridors,
Guarded by the English custom of suspicion.

And to prove my situation
I have written this, so that

When they have fingered their
Dirty hands through my clothes,
Mauled my enjoyable flight
With personal questions,
Pricked a little for reaction,
And arrived at my book, I will point them to this poem
Simply to tell them
That I get job satisfaction, in the end,
And they will get nothing but tobacco beneath their nails.

Mind-Walking

A stray sunshot caught
His heart.

As a child
He spent time
Melting,
   Dripping,
Like a fallen lolly on a kerb
In summer.

As a child
He teased questions from his
Black-topped brain,
Like he'd
Lick the bowl when his mother left
The kitchen.

There was always one ultimate question
That arose
While building
Mud pies,
Or staring at cobwebs in hedges.

Only as the full line itched his tongue,
As it had unravelled from his thoughts like a red carpet,
Only when the gravity of his question became its heaviest,
Unbearable almost,
Would he race home and
Stand with the urgency
Of a young boy desperate for a pee.
'Mum, Mum.'

Who was doing the same thing as he
But in the kitchen,
'If the earth is
          Spinning why doesn't it move
          If I jump up and
Why aren't I dizzy . . .?'

A stray sunshot caught
Her heart.

She would call it
Brain-strolling or mind-walking,
Said he'd walk into church
One day and say,
'Why is God not here?'
On receiving a stiff reply,
He'd look at the cross and say,
'Well, he doesn't have to hang about like that.
He can have my seat.'

2

A stray sunshot bled into
His heart.

          Welled in his chest,
          Crept up the inside of his eyelids,

Curdled through his whip-like lashes,
Down the bright brown bony cheeks.

          He had run till his breath
          Was almost too far ahead of him.

He had run till his heartbeat
Had overtaken his pounding feet,

Till the rustle of the trees
Had taken his breath,

Till the squawk of a magpie
Had overtaken the rustle of the trees,

Till the rattle of the keys
Had overtaken the squawk of a magpie.

He had run till his breath
Was almost too far ahead of him.
It filled the kitchen, and his mother
Listened to it counting
Four hundred years
Of panting.
She heard her
Grandfather in him,
Her grandmother's wheeze,
Her father's defiance,
Her husband's private sobbing
At being broken.
She listened until
The room was filled with spirits
Ricocheting from wall to wall,
Cradled in the sink
Dripping from the ceiling.
Clinging to their necks like weak motherless children . . .

Here was a question he would ask them,
And it would twist their bodies each time.

For My Headstone

Here is the death of the son you never had,
The hand you never touched,
The face you never stroked.

Here is the morning after,
His bruises you never tended,
The laughter you never shared.

And here are the tears he'll never feel,
Your eyes he'll never see,
Whispers he'll never hear.
The apologies
Will squirm in his coffin
With the letters you never wrote.

Love Poem

You remind me,
Define me,
Incline me.

If you died
I'd.

Flowers in the Kitchen

On buying her flowers
She said,

'There's no food in the kitchen
And we can't eat flowers.'

On buying her food
She said,

'You don't buy flowers any more.'

Suitcases and Muddy Parks

You say I am a lying child.
I say I'm not.
You say there you go again.

You say I am a rebellious child.
I say no, I'm not.
You say there you go again.

Quite frankly, Mum,
I've never seen a rebellious child before.
And when my mates said,
Jump in that puddle and race you through the park
(y'know the muddy one),
I didn't think about the mud.

When you said why are you dirty?!
I could feel the anger in your voice.
I still don't know why.

I said I raced my mates through the park.
You said it was deliberate.
I said I didn't . . . I mean, I did . . . but it wasn't.
You said I was lying.
I said no, I'm not.
You said there you go again.

Later in the dawn of adolescence
It was time for my leave,
I with my suitcase and social worker,
You with your husband.
We walked our sliced ways.

Sometimes I run back to you
Like a child through a muddy park,
Adult achievements tucked under my arm.

I explain them with a childlike twinkle,
Thinking any mother would be proud.

Your eyes desperately trying to be wise and unrevealing
        reveal all.
Still you fall back into the same rocking chair,
        Saying there you go again.

And I did.
And I have.

The Nest

In shells
Small bells
Echo
Echoes

Till the hairline crack
Hisses

Revealing
Small chickens.

That's us:
Small chickens
Learning to hatch.

Different eggs
In the same nest.

Pass It On

How is it that we still smile when the pressure comes?
How is it that we stand firm when they think that we should
  run?
How is it that we retain our integrity?
How is it through this maze that we keep the clarity?
How is it that through pain we retain compassion?
How is it that we spread but stay one nation?
How is it that we work in the face of abuse?
How is it that the pressure's on yet we seem loose?
This is the story about the rising truth,
When you feel closed in simply raise the roof.
The Africans were the first civilisation,
Born by the Nile was the first generation.

Malcolm X had a dream, we have a dream too,
And the only way to get it is to pass it on through,
From the day we leave to the day we arrived
We were born to survive, born to stay alive,
By all means necessary I'm an accessory,
To provide the positive vibe is a necessity,
To clasp our past to go to war with our fears,
To claim and attain in our future years.
Sometimes life can be cold and complicated;
More times the problem is overrated.
Nina Simone called it the Backlash Blues,
Even though they say it's history, we all know that it's news.

The oppressor hopes and prays for you to cry,
To close your hearts and your minds to lay down and die,
To be another numb number to treat and delete,
To fall into the spiral rhythm of defeat.
Malcolm X had a dream, we have a dream too,
And the only way to get it is to pass it on through.
No message has been stronger, no sea carried more weight,
No army marched for longer, no wind swept at this rate.

So pride in my skin is in the vision I have seen,
The pain I withstand for I have a dream.
Know who you are, know the ground on which you stand.
Never build your house on a bed of sand.

Going Places

Another
Cigarette ash,
Television serial-filled,
Advert-analysing,
Cupboard-starving,
Front room-filling,
Tea-slurping,
Mind-chewing,
Brain-burping,
Carpet-picking,
Pots watching,
Room-gleaning,
Toilet-flushing
Night,
With nothing to do.

I think I'll paint roads
On my front room walls
To convince myself
That I'm going places.

Gil Scott-Heron

Gil Scott-Heron shines
In tightly cut rhythmic rhymes.

The Harlem hero strikes again,
Jazz in the house, milk the pain.

From politics in poetics,
The symbols in the lyrics

Shut in the drum ripple in the skin
While the bass dives deep and digs in.

Gil Scott-Heron shines
In tightly cut rhythmic rhymes.

The Washington wonder strikes again,
Jazz in the house, milk the pain.

And Brian Jackson in zoot suit
Places into the root the sweet flute,

Black and in Britain we know what Scott means
When he documents the siege of New Orleans,

With subtlety in vibes and lyrics giving clues,
The man talks in colours in the inner city blues,

Explained how television would not be revolutionised
And how the revolution would not be televised.

This panther is black, catch its silhouette,
Cutting a shadow to outline the debt.

Martin Luther King and a cut of Malcolm X
Wrapped in the musical strength of the Amnesia Express.

Gil Scott-Heron shines
In tightly cut rhythmic lines.

Another black hero strikes again,
Jazz in the house, milk the pain.

Godsell

You knock upon my door
And open.
I drink to you.
This is a bad trip,
Something about Armageddon
And pigs possessed by devils
Flinging themselves from cliffs.
Look back into my house and I may turn to salt.

Blackened horizons itch with locusts,
Whole pieces of earth slump
Swallowed by the devil's breath;
Yea, as I walk through the valley of death
With Lucifer in the crick of my back,
An avalanche of commands befalls me,
And I whimper from the cross and catapult
In the child's hand,
Clutching a lock of my own hair,
Feeling the heat of a burning bush
Singe the back of my neck.
Three score and ten years of this;
Look back into my house and I may turn to salt.

Where is the chariot of fire?
Where is the chariot of fire?
I, one piece of thirty pieces of silver,
A possessed pig, laugh at the cliff's edge,
Snort and fling myself to the rocks.
When I meet Peter
I shall bribe him,
As I have been bribed.

Flushed

Why
Can't
Heads
Have
Overflow pipes
      Like toilets?
      If
      They
      Did
      I
      Could
      Pull
      My
      Ear
      And
      Flush
      It
      All
      Out.

I Hate You

You're as popular as a posted
Birthday gift to someone who's just died.
I once said you weren't that bad,
I lied.

You're a conversation number,
Your presence binds lips together.
Why is it when your name is mentioned
There's a sudden change of weather?

You're a lift to a claustrophobic,
A witch to a priest.
You're gushy and gooey.
You're my release.

I wouldn't be a bell ringer
With a face like that.
Here, see how hard you can
Head butt this cricket bat.

How can we discuss the meaning of life
When you don't deserve it?
It's a bad habit that, breathing,
I wish you could curb it.

It's short and sweet,
And there isn't much pain.
Have you ever tried hang-gliding
Without a plane?

I'd say I didn't mean all this,
But truthfully I'd be lying,
And I really wouldn't write it
If I thought that you'd be crying.

In fact if I was you I wouldn't
See any need for resentment,
Because from me to you, quite honestly,
This has got to be a compliment.

Professional Black

Whirlwinds attract you more than the common breeze.
It's too easy to see the wood and never the trees.
You can make a tailor-made struggle just for the stage,
And the government will fund it 'cause it's all the rage.

And you can fool the bodies into giving you the readies,
Because only black people can define just where your head is.
When I check it out the hammer hits upon the nail.
You speak about the struggle as if it was a fairy tale.

As if it was a vehicle, your personal limousine,
With closed and tinted windows to take you to your dream,
And the only ones who see this are the ones who realise
That you're cheating this 'community' with lies.

You disagree with these words and theatrically deny,
Telling me what you've done for black people, never telling me
    why.
And there before my eyes it became totally apparent
That you were never black – you were simply transparent.

Pretoria Pit

I lived next to Pretoria,
A deformed tongue of earth,
Holding fathers and sons in clenched stone throats.

Young estate kids stole motorbikes,
Wheel-spinning on the fossilised spines of miners
Who groaned in the trips of hippies
Who plucked magic mushrooms from their mouths.

In parts, on sharp sides, silver birches scream for light
Like the flame-breathing canaries.
Pretoria bleeds in still pond pockets.

And I'd sit on this and watch the sun through
The dead mill windows; make it look
Like a church, like it was crying,
Like the whole Lancashire plain was mourning
As the souls rose through the birch trees
And suckled the stars.

Our estate hunched at Pretoria's feet,
Fell down from there,
As if in awe,
As if running away down into the village,
Desperate to break through onto Market Street.

Uncle Tom and the 1990s

The way he
Bowed his head to the lilac princess
And spat on the young black boy

Polished his shoes and ignored the news
Of the lynching in his own backyard,

Or folded his clothes and held up his nose
At the sounds of a screaming sister:

Uncle Tom, the same syllable sound
As true or false, sweet and sour,
Right or wrong, do or die,

Is dead,
Manacled mutilated moaning in his grave,
Twisting and turning in all the suppressed unrest.

He sweeps the floors of hell,
Licks the walls of heaven,
Takes all the sinners to the pit of eternal fire,
Children, crinkly old men, crimson young girls;
Holds them by the hand, tells them
They'll be all right, they'll get used to it, and hums,

'Oh Lordy, pick a bale of souls
Oh Lordy, pick a bale a day
Gonna jump down turn around pick a bale of souls
Everydoghasitsdayhewholivestorunawayifatfirstyoudon't
succeedabirdinthehandisbettereyesbiggerthanyouranger
begatsangerdon'trocktheboat.'

Frustrated black people still pull him from the grave,
But the myth
Has decomposed and doesn't hold together
The years between then and now.

We are at the crux of making
A martyr from a fool,
A fool from a martyr.

Uncle Tom is dead.
Hot oil spittle pours from each orifice
His solidified words
'Everycloudhasathere'sgoodandbadinweareallthesameunder . . .
      liveandletlive.'

Make him a saint or a swear word;
Both are a modern-day charade.

There is no Uncle Tom in the 1990s;
Just cold calculated black moving sculptures, sharp and sinister,
Who know exactly what they're doing.

Clear as Day Storms

It's in the secluded moment
Or the hectic deadlines
That beyond my control
I remember the times
When skies bent with red strength,
To protect our innocent minds,
Would paint pathways home
For memories to find.

But moon-soaked storms
(As we swam against the tide
or circled like eagles
above the mountain sides)
Dragged me
Into the hurricane's eye
And sucked me through
Darkened skies;

Through ricocheted demands,
Commands too high to reach,
Grey rooms, rattling keys,
And corridors too bleached.
With no space to breathe
I would sit by the window pane
To watch the storm stabbing
And the night-time cry in pain.

And now in the night's whisper
And the single magpie's lull,
As the air thick and humid
And the wind begins to pull,
I greet the storm,
Stand in its rain,
And somehow you're as clear
As the day again.

My Brother

We laughed, played draughts,
Under a sweeping sleeping sun
By the coconut tree
And the smell of lemon grass.
He had returned from Paris.

It took us half an hour
To get the right coconut
And two minutes to mix the juice
With raspberry cordial.
That night I cried,
How alike we could have been.

Children and Company

It's children who spot sand-pits
And large puddles,
Insect spit
And warm cuddles.

It's children who spot spiders
And dew-cobbled cobwebs,
Holes in bushes
And worms that are half dead.

It's children who spot puddles,
Pavement cracks and kerbs,
cement between bricks
And brand new verbs.

It's children who spot Granddad
Picking at his nose,
The stubble on his chin,
The smell on his clothes.

It's children who spot shadows
Disguised as monsters
And brown knotty sticks
To chuck at the conkers.
It's children who spot scruffy dogs
And skinny cats,
And bird nests in the tweed
of an old flat cap.

It's children who spot broken-legged blackbirds
And the biggest caterpillar,
The one with the fangs
That had to be a killer.

Writer's Blockocks

Instead of rolling my tongue around a juicy adjective
While finding myself an abstract objective
To metaphorically master through a perfect perspective
And economically edit to its utmost connective,
I find myself lost in a cell full of words.
I know what I want to do but I can't find the verbs.
Rhymes are on the run through the keyhole and under the
    door,
Saying I am going to die a death if you use me any more.

But a padded cell is not enough, it's another cliché.
Another padded-out and poached piece of poetry today.
My illness is spreading, pathetic as the odd sock,
Or the fact that gets me to the rhyme – I've got writer's block.
Grief wells, haunting my paper with cunning and clarity,
To see this block, the big full stop, the end to my literacy.
Suicide seems to be the only recurring choice
For on top of all this, I'm an oral poet and I think I'm losing
    my voice!

LIVERPOOL JOHN MOORES UNIVERSITY
LEARNING SERVICES

The Black Moon

Some would say there was no moon
If it was black, because it can't be seen
With the naked eye,
Like there is a naked eye
Unattached to a brain.

I would say take a closer look.
Here, use this telescope,
Point it towards that star.
Yes, the white and bright one.
Can you relate to that? Right,
Now move it to the left . . . up a little.

An outline, a circular shape.
That's the one, yeah! Yes, that's the black moon.
A circular magnificence reveals and breathes
Itself into another mind, free again.
The music of knowing.

Taking his eye away,
Quizzically, mockingly, he said,
'Yeah, but what do I want to know that for?'

All that investigation
All that proof –
For what?
Think I'll use my energy showing
A black man a black moon.

Brinkley Park

In the interval of each footstep
A distant drunken couple laugh.
Like a lioness chewing gravel,
Her feet crunched the speckled path.
Thinking of every memory-hugging
Short cut she knew so well,
She waited as walking for the
Timely chime of the 3 a.m. church bell.
As she recalled the warmth
Of pillow and sheet,
She slowly bent under the shadow of the willow
To rub awake her sleeping feet,
And it was cold, wet
And dauntingly dark,
As she stepped through
The bowels of Brinkley Park.

The trees, dew-slimy as the beads
Of sweat on the face of the killer.
The mist clung to oak and grass,
Like a scene from a midnight thriller.
Yet this was a far cry from
Any television show,
As were her treacle tears with
Each life-sapping blow.
Shadows ripped the grass verges
Into vast empty ravines,
Vast and empty enough to
Swallow her muffled screams.
He acted out his illness,
Gas to his hallucinated spark,
The day he raped Charla Leeston
In the bowels of Brinkley Park.

And another woman fell victim
To the penis wrapped in barbed wire.
Another woman withdrew into the attic,
Seeing smoke and in fear of the fire.
Another woman wraps herself
Into one piece of clothing more,
And another woman finds
The thirteenth bolt for her security door.

Rage

Take the sea in handfuls
And spill it onto this city's streets,
And no one will notice at first.
Vagrants will laugh into the bottle,
Builders will point from the scaffolding,
Intellects will snort in mid-conversation,
Office workers will glance through windows.

Taking the sea in handfuls is not a loud task.
I may sing while I am doing it.
I may skip while carrying.
I am allowed.

The glances and snorts irritate.
'Yeah – it's the sea, ha!'
It feels so triumphant to let it
Trickle through my fingers into the cracked kerbs.

MORNING BREAKS IN THE ELEVATOR

The Waitress and the Nights of the Round Table

Each immaculate table a near perfect reflection of the next;
A '40s Hollywood formation dance captured in time –
In black and white.
On the mahogany, polished as a morning pond,
Each tablecloth flapped as swan's wings,
And each landing perfect.
She made pieces of butter, intricate
As the hand-woven curls in a judge's wig.
And if not so legal and final
They'd be a crest of waves
Caught in yellow sunshine.

Each serviette a silent smiling cygnet born in her hands,
Each flower arranged as if grown for this evening
Sucks water slowly through the stem and raises its neck.
They bathe in the light flitting from a cut crystal vase
And stand assertive in centre tables, waiting.
She picks a speck of dust from a spotless unspeckled carpet.
Her reflection buckles in the neck of a mercurial fork
While the solemn red candles wait
To weep their red tears.

She pauses as a mother would for a moment
In the front room, before the visitors arrive,
In admiration and slight concern,
And bathes in the symmetry and silence
And the oddness of order –
Even the tables seem to brace themselves as she leaves.
The picture was distorted when she returned from the kitchen.
A hungry horde of steak-sawing, wine-guzzling,
Spirit-sapping double-breasted suits had grabbed their places.
They dug their spiked elbows into the wilting backs of tables.
The tablecloth dripped congealed red wine from its quiet
    hanging corners

And the sounds of their grunts, growls, their slurping,
Their gulping and tearing invaded the hall.

But a black swan amongst a sea of serrated cutlery, she soared
    just above
And wove a delicate determined ballet in between – invisible.
She walked for miles that evening, balancing platters,
Pinafore-perfect hair clipped so not to slip.
The wine warmed and the candles cried.

In the background of the lashings of laughter –
The guttural sound of wolves.
She retrieved a carcass of lamb, poured red,
And didn't notice the bloodshot eyes slide over her:
Nor the claws stretching and puncturing leather brogues;
Scratching the wooden floor; nor their irritation at her.
One mauled a mobile phone with a clumsy paw,
The alcohol-fuelled change was taking hold.
And together they could be and become who they really were.
Wolves. Wolves in their pride. Wolves in their pack.
Their lower jaws had stretched and eyes slitted –
Some even bayed as wolves, heads flicking side to side,
Tongues slipping low, slow and deliberately from their mouths
And curling sensually to their snouts. The wolf has a
    permanent smile.
It grew, first half-cough, half-bark. One paw banged on the
    table,
Another banged and another and another and another

Until the whole hall echoed with the unified clatter
Of the guttural phlegm-flicked word that brought them together
'Gerni gerni gerni gerni,' they chanted.'Ggerni ggerni ggerni,'
    they chanted faster.
'Ggerni Ggerni Ggerni Ggerni,' faster and faster.
'GgernigGerniggerniGgerniggerniggeriggernigger.'

She turned to her colleagues who stood by the kitchen entrance,
But their eyes! Their eyes slipped sideways away from her.

They too were wolves! Her lips parted for her voice and the
    room hushed itself,
But for the slipping of saliva from their jaws and the flickering
    candles
And the dripping of the red wine from the tablecloth.
As instructed by her manager, she, smiling politely,
Asked a wolf, 'More coffee, sir?'

Colour Blind

If you can see the sepia in the sun,
Shades of grey in fading streets,
The radiating bloodshot in a child's eye,
The dark stains in her linen sheets.

If you can see oil separate on water,
The turquoise of leaves on trees,
The reddened flush of your lover's cheeks,
The violet peace of calmed seas.

If you can see the bluest eye,
The purple in the petals of the rose,
The blue anger, the venom, of the volcano,
The creeping orange of the lava flows.

If you can see the red dust of the famished road,
The white airtight strike of Nike's sign.
If you can see the skin tone of a Lucien Freud,
The colours of his frozen subject in mime.

If you can see the white mist of the oasis,
The red, white and blue that you defended.
If you can see it all through the blackest pupil,
The colours stretching, the rainbow suspended.

If you can see the breached blue of the evening,
And the caramel curls in the swirls of your tea,
Why do you say you are colour blind
When you see me?

Charlie's Playing Blackjack

(For David Murray)

It's got to scream like a thousand shivers.
Shake down, break down, run like rivers of black fire-waves.
Rise demons and spirits from the Senegalese caves.
Rise Beloved *and* Seth! Rise the dead!
For this sound digs, digs down-down where the deep down
Is down with the deep down till it reaches the beaches of
      Goree.
Until it stabs-stabs as it grab-grabs the minute minute. Hold
      fast.
It flows through passages, right, like a flock of carrion crows,
And stings and blows and stings and blows,
Makes sadness sing high and swing low.
SWEET CHARIOTS OF FIRE!

Quotes wrapped in rolled notes, stick into the spokesmen's
      eyes.
The hoaxmen of the mainstream deep scream.
Deep, Davis, deep. So deep, Davis, I can't sleep for the
Sweeping sounds of your underground. This landscape
Littered with mounds. Rise, Spirits, rise. Uncoil. Break the soil –
The bread of the dead, the salt of the earth. Rise
And flow like mercurial contours on a midnight sky. Cry.
Till the tears solidify. Fly, Spirits, till you become a song.
Eye to eye. Right to wrong. Untie pain. Dance again
Till juices jive down your scarred backbones.
This is the other world – *live* – and yet home.

This sound electrifies, soars on the edge of the head.
Waken the dead and tell them it's here – 'it's here',
For duppies to wind and spirits to near home – at last.
To brutify, then purify, then reunify the past.
Rise, Malcolm, the Jews, the blues and the Soledad brothers.
Shout. Bleed. Breathe. Heal. Shout. Breathe. Heal. Bleed.

I swear I saw another slave freed, its soul freed, it gather speed,
Pushing me over the edge of the ledge, dredging the graveyards,
The Spirits – Charlie's playing cards on the tomb, a dead man's
    womb.

Don't you get it. It's genetic. A musical hallucinogenic. Insane –
The music of love through the instruments of pain,
Shooting from the lip, from the tip of the tongues of the
    wronged.
Hang on, hang on with your finger tips. Pray you don't slip,
'Cause we climbing the timing, the landscape of mine.
Turn this poem sideways, it's like a New York skyline,
A state of mind.

And through to the solo light. Right. Solo.
How does it go? It glides like an eagle inches from the waves,
With a rush that sounds like caves should sound like.
It rips through all mind-binds, breaks all seals, tears all
    seems – seams,
Chilled as fresh-iced screams, angry as sweated dreams.
It bites like a baby, kicks like a dog, slicker than a card trick.
Demons spit and twist as spirits hit notes high (ha!) and snare.
This is where contrasts explode and it's natural to find
Sharpness next to curves, next to shadows, next to verve,
And new definitions of time. It is the blood of the vein.
The music of love through the instruments of pain.

Hot cold shy bold rock rolled blue soul. Rise!
Makes an old man young, a young girl old. Rise!
It's a slick wild blast, cast from chains of slaves.

I found my jazz. Rise. I found my jazz. Rise.
I found my jazz and was saved.
Rise, Spirits.

Invisible Kisses

If there was ever one
Whom when you were sleeping
Would wipe your tears
When in dreams you were weeping;
Who would offer you time
When others demand;
Whose love lay more infinite
Than grains of sand.

If there was ever one
To whom you could cry;
Who would gather each tear
And blow it dry;
Who would offer help
On the mountains of time;
Who would stop to let each sunset
Soothe the jaded mind.

If there was ever one
To whom when you run
Will push back the clouds
So you are bathed in sun;
Who would open arms
If you would fall;
Who would show you everything
If you lost it all.

If there was ever one
Who when you achieve
Was there before the dream
And even then believed;
Who would clear the air
When it's full of loss;
Who would count love
Before the cost.

If there was ever one
Who when you are cold
Will summon warm air
For your hands to hold;
Who would make peace
In pouring pain,
Make laughter fall
In falling rain.

If there was ever one
Who can offer you this and more;
Who in keyless rooms
Can open doors;
Who in open doors
Can see open fields
And in open fields
See harvests yield.

Then see only my face
In the reflection of these tides
Through the clear water
Beyond the river side.
All I can send is love,
In all that this is
A poem and a necklace
Of invisible kisses.

Slipping

You
Are
Slipping
Away.
Don't
Go if you want to.
See if I need you.
You
Are
Slipping
Away.
Don't
Leave if you want to.
See if I miss you.

        You
        Are
        Slipping
        Away.
        Don't
        Call if you want to.
        See if I miss you.

                Slipping
                Slipping
                Don't
                Wave if you want to.
                See if I care, for you
                        Are
                        Slipping
                        Slipping
                        Slipping
                        Away.

Murdering Bill

With less than the pressure
Of a downpressing butterfly wing in a feather field –
The opening of an eyelid would make more noise –
He opened the letterbox so slowly that it was
As unsuspecting as a passing yawn in the morning.
A smooth criminal face tattooed with blue ink
With *my* name peers. This Royal Male,
The silent secret stalker, crouched delicately
Outside the front door – eyes filled the letterbox
Like two greedy gulping goldfish in a tank.

He drinks in the shadows of the sleeping hall
And becoming almost liquidite
Squeezes savagely through the letterbox
Arms first, head stretched, ears cut.
Now he has the eyes and the body of a lizard
The strain written in blue veins on his face
He pulls through the legs and he is in.

A lizard. He waits for breath to calm and becomes
Cold and camouflaged. Digging his elbows into carpet
He slides into the front room where I am
Enveloped in the Saturday paper. Turn a page,
This is my affidavit, this is what happened.
I saw him. I read the look in his eyes and he read mine.
He laughed at me. Stood on his hind legs and spat at me.

His tongue slipping from his mouth like a serrated ribbon,
There he is lying in the centre of my front room.
Slumped from my clammy clumsy hands,
Back to the floor limp, his head and legs bent.
I've been here transfixed since. Staring at him.
Waiting for him to die – but he breathes, he breathes.
As many times as I twist his damned throat he breathes.

Immigration R.S.V.P.

The lemons you suck are from Spain,
And the orange you drink's from South Africa.
Shoes you wear are made in Pakistan,
And your oil is from Saudi Arabia.

You import your petrol from the Gulf States,
And your toys are made in Taiwan.
Your coffee they send from Colombia,
And your cars are driven from Japan.

You've flooded yourself with foreign good,
But foreigners you tell me are bad.
You say you're afraid that they'll overrun you,
But I'm afraid they already have.

Fair

I'll rein in then chain you in.
I'll slit, whip and rip into you,
Till all the cold as nitric acid resentment
Pours out of my black chest
Onto your purpled, curdled and blistered back.
I'll whip you till you howl and crawl and cry.
I'll pour salt in your mouth, rub shit in your eyes,
Pour vinegar into the canals of your ears.
I'll verify all your superficial fears

I'll wrench each finger from each joint
Till you get my point. Get it. Get my point!
I'll drag you by the roots of your hair –
Make you wish you were no one from nowhere.
Show you what it's like on the other side;
Show you what it's like on the far side.
My knuckle-dusted fists will rein down,
Busting veins will curse,
Blow after bitter blow.
I'll ask you how it feels,
I'm doing a thesis, I'd really like to know.

I'll cut you a thousand times
While repeating the line,
'Yes, I know, your blood is red like mine.'
I'll rip out your wife's fallopian tubes
'Cause there's already too many of you.
I'll make you drink your own hiss,

I'll make you listen to this,
One, two, three thousand times and more,
Show you what it's like to know the score.
I'll sell drugs to your children,
Burn down your home,
Make you a stranger to your own.

And what's more,
The moment you run on fire,
Through this poem, for the door,
Gasping for air and some sense of pride,
The same damned experience
Will be waiting for you outside.

I haven't finished . . .
When it dawns that this scorning
Is sworn in and government-approved,
When the pattern starts to emerge,
And you're on the verge of enlightenment or madness,
Immersed in the quiet violence of the day-to-day laws,
When you notice the holder of the mirror has claws
And the reflection provided is disfigured and displaced,
When your tongue splits on the bitter taste,
When your head implodes,
Because the text between the lines
Is so suffocating that you've started reading minds,
When all this is said and done and said and done,
You may accuse me of being a racist
And that we can continue 'this discussion'
On a more equal basis!

The Repossession: Lot 67

A girl clasped by the sinews of vicious storms
Of saliva spat through sanctimonious scorn.

Gossip gathered in teacups and tapping tea spoons.
'How dare a woman bear such waste in her womb?'

They locked her in the watchtower for husbandless women
And counted her debt in the cells that were splitting.

Forced her to bathe by night in tin tubs of guilt,
Or be damned to the sewer's side with the skeleton silt.

They pressured her each day to study Mary Immaculate in
     pastel pictures,
Made her eat the dead and dry daily bread of water and
     scriptures.

And no sooner had the secrets of birth found her
Than the hospital curtains crept around her.

No sooner had air swilled in virgin lungs and seeped through
     the critical mesh
Than they thumped their fists into her and gripped their
     pound of flesh.

Bathed in blood. Without pressure the womb weak and
     depressed.
Miss, the bailiff growled, your child has been repossessed.

Baptism in Mire

As the pastor dragged the 'forgiven'
From that watery grave
They'd say 'Jesus Christ'
And he'd shout 'You are saved'.

My F. parents 'chastised' me
For the way that I frowned.
They thought me possessed by the devil;
I thought they were being drowned.

Controlled Explosions

Picked up in anticipation and dropped in greater
    disappointment
By distressed couples searching for their own intimate luggage.
The suitcase has been tampered with and rummaged through,
Doesn't know where it's come from nor where it's going to.
Its dog-eared flight-tags lost in streams of weaving conveyor
    belts,
Its broken zips' open lips too tired to beg the desperate duets.
Ham-fisted and impatient, they fumble inside the hammered
    leather,
Finding in someone else's belongings an unforgiving
    unfamiliarity.
They wash their hands clinically, forget about mending it,
    and disappear.

As time passes the suitcase becomes battered and bruised,
Stubbornly jamming the conveyor belts at the airport,
Reminding families to grip their suitcases and step politely over
Before guilt or fear sets in. Someone reports the problem,
Tannoys whisper, security arrives. Order and authority
    descends,
Causing disorder and panic amongst the passing.

This case is the lost cargo of international departures.
With broken zips and hidden padlocked dust-collecting pockets,
It may explode, for all we know, at any time.
Carefully, cordons are placed around the area.
To make sure everyone is covered.
All the conveyor belts grind to a mournful halt.
The airport gathers quietness and a sweeping hush blows.
Outside a professional looks confidently to camera. It's news!
I've been reliably informed the controlled explosion shall
    begin shortly.

Children's Home

The children nearby came to our secret garden,
Gazed at our mansion in disbelief,
Either said they wished they lived here
Or that this was the den of the thief.
But it was our Narnia of food fights at midnight,
Wet flannel battles in the halls,
Fire extinguishers that lose their heads.
We had nothing to lose – nothing at all.

But the rattle of rules and keys
Broke the magic – we all knew it couldn't last.
The alarm bells rang and rang and rang
In Emergency Break The Glass
And it's no fun any more in here.
The keys in cupboards, slamming security doors,
Each child slowly retracts inside their self,
Whispering, 'What am I being punished for?'

We'd been given booby-trapped time-bombs,
Trigger wires hidden, strapped on the inside.
It became a place of controlled explosions,
Self-mutilation, screams and suicide,
Of young people returned, return to sender.
Half-light dorms of midnight's moans –
We might well have all been children
But this was never a children's home.

Walking in Circles

These compressed patches of earth.
Her footsteps deepened
And I found myself, raising my knee
To follow in them,
Raising my elbows
To climb over them,
Bracing myself
To jump in them.
Who was she
That left imprints
Deeper than myself?

Wiping sweat from the crease
Between cheek and nose
With a dirty hand, I
Mumble, why so deep?
Wait for me.
Why so deep?

Later I realised
That without meeting
We'd been walking
In circles, stamping our imprints.
Every now and then I would
Hear her wheezing, trying to climb
Over her own imprint
And jump into the next.

My Dad Is a Pilot

My dad is a pilot. Everybody knows that.
He wore a green pilot's suit and he wore a pilot's hat.
He was never more at home, he was never more free
Than flying past the cities or skimming past the sea.

He flew past the Simien mountains, past even the stars.
He flew far my dad did. He flew far.
He flew past Ethiopia of night and of day.
He passed my past. He flew right past
And then he passed away.

Guilt

Cold winds have frozen us,
Walls of fear closed on us.

The sky has fallen down on us,
And fear it has frowned on us.

The lightning has dumbfounded us,
A dust cloud surrounded us.

The rain it pours down on us,
Pain has been found on us.

Secrets they have bound us,
Anointed and then crowned us.

Whispers race around us,
Fingers point down on us.

Fists beat and pound on us,
Our reflections astound us.

Fear it compounds us,
Defences surround us.

Frustrations hound us,
Guilt has found us.

Sandwich Love

Triangular sandwiches lounge on plates.
They don't guffaw, gawp or gesticulate.
They kiss each other lip to salivating lip.
They don't posture, pose and stylishly sip.
They don't have calling cards, and though well dressed
Have no need or will for public address.
They just pout at each other, smile and wink.
They go down well with drink.

Triangular sandwiches all love-struck.
Have you ever seen a more glazed blushing cook?
'Slap me with the salmon and pull down the shutters.'
'Smother me in butter,' another one mutters.
'Stroke me down with cucumber slices . . . '
'I like it like that, pepper me with spices.'
'Massage that cream cheese over my chest.'
'Let your olive oil seep through my bread vest.'

Triangular sandwiches soaked in salad dressing.
The lusciously laid lovers among the depressing.
Pretenders pretending they're enjoying the chat.
Of the who's who in the what's what of where it must be at.
The lush lounge lizards lay and, like when lovers undo,
Stretch by the rosed radish as corks seductively unscrew.
But a suit will saunter his hand, will swoop limply from above.
He will open his salivating mouth, push one in and shove.
He will crunch her inside his grating teeth
And leave the other sandwich sandwiched in grief.

The Elevator

It was embarrassing for him. I sixth-sensed it. Me.
One hotel. One elevator. One world. Two people.
One black. One white. One young. One old.
One thousand conflicting thoughts.
One silence. One destination.
For one it was a short journey,
For one it was long.
With one nervy question
He just had to break the silence.
'Are you with the basketball team?'
I answer choosing a two-lettered
One-syllable staccato reply:
'No.'

As he mentally rocked to and fro, swilling in discomfort,
The elevator hummed like it was listening into the atmosfear.
Instead of thinking that I might slam dunk his head through
A hoop that had spit for a net, I drift.
I imagine the elevator gracefully passing the ground floor,
As an eagle might pass a parachutist
Who couldn't find his rip cord.
It continues to go down deeper and deeper
Down where the deeper down is.
Where deep is down with deeper down.
Down.

A Flock of Sound

There is a rhythm, a soul's rhythm,
A come in from the cold rhythm,
A no need to go rhythm,
A take off your bruise shoes
And shake off tomorrow rhythm.
There is a rhythm, a wild rhythm,
An adult's just a child rhythm,
A blissed-out whispering
Smile while listening rhythm.

There is a rhythm, a higher than sky rhythm.
The rhythm of spaces, a sweet-tasting,
Liquor-laced rhythm. An eyelid-flicking,
Slick thigh-licking rhythm.
A come home to the comfort zone rhythm.
A relax in your black, take nothing back rhythm.

There is a rhythm, a rhythm.
A sweet-sounding grounded rhythm,
A spaced-out sense of place rhythm,
A give in to your within rhythm,
A rainy season body-teasing,
Dripping sugar-caned cocooned,
Landing on the moon rhythm.
A making-room rhythm.

A lake and mist lip-kissing dew-glistening,
Earthed and wired surround-sound future-bound,
Magic-carpeted and homeward bound rhythm.
A pain-soothing hip-moving pressure-releasing
Depression-decreasing graffiti-wriggling baby-
Giggling Zebra crossing – Walk Don't Walk – button-pressing
Up town, down town dressing spirit-shaking earth-quaking

Ripples in a lake of a rhythm.
Ripples in a lake of a rhythm.
Ripples in a lake.
A flock of sound.

The Graduate and Her Secret Thesis

It was the evening before the eve of her deadline.
They made love between the sheets of her thesis.
After taking a shower of words she sat at the table
And studied him through the book pile, turned over leaves;
She perfected paragraphs punctuated with references,
Glue to stick the whole thing together.
Two thousand five hundred words to go.

In her mind she had passed the exam already,
But at the same time her pencil snapped
Like the cracking of a twig signifying an intruder.
A problem. It stalked her thoughts, scared her.
That stubborn sentence if not justified would turn into a
    tapeworm, a gremlin,
Eat the whole thesis and belch in her face.
We engaged and I followed her delicate fingers
Along that snare-riddled trigger-wired sentence.
She read it again and again in the voice of a question,
Finding new angles each time and new meanings
That refer to previous explanations in other books
That neither of us had at the time.
She stared at me for the answer and I at her.
This was going to take work – more work than either expected.
Midnight.

In the whisk of a page, the thud of a dropped book,
We entered the old university reference library.
The closing doors behind us sent
A gust of air dust curling and searching
Down the corridors of books like a flock of grey swans.
The night light shone a red brown.
I noticed how different she looked – nervous almost –
Her caramel skin more beautiful than usual.
I've since forgotten who'd said let's split up and search but
    we did.

The Bruise

I got the bruise, the bruise,
Since before I was born.
Bruise is the only clothing
That I've ever worn.

I got the bruise, the bruise,
Nothing no doctor can do.
Don't come near me, woman,
'Cause I'm sure gonna bruise you too.

I got the bruise in my flesh,
The bruise deep and dark.
I got the bruise all over my face, my arms,
My head, my soul 'n' my heart.

I get so drunk I get bruises on my bruise,
And that ain't no disguise.
I got the bruise, I got the bruise,
I got the bruise in my eyes.
I got the bruise, I got the bruise,
I got the bruise in my eyes.

Quiet Places

Some people on bus seats shake at the shoulders,
Stoned Elvises trying to dance after the gig.

Some walk into the rain and look like they're smiling,
Running mascara writes sad bitter letters on their faces.

Some drive their cars into lay-bys or park edges
And cradle the steering-wheel looking like headless drivers.

Some sink their open mouths into feather pillows
And tremble on the bed like beached dolphins.

Some people are bent as question marks when they weep
And some are straight as exclamation marks.

Some are soaking in emotional dew when they wake,
Salt street maps etched into their faces.

Some find rooms and fall to the floor as if praying to Allah.
  Noiseless
Faces contorted in that silent scream that seems like laughter.

Why is there not a tissue-giver? A man who looks for tears,
Who makes the finest silk tissues and offers them for free?

It seems to me that around each corner, beneath each stone,
Are humans quietly looking for a place to cry on their own.

Mourning Breaks

They always said I was over the edge
And now I am. I really am over the edge!
But as I dropped, in a gasp of air, I grasped a branch
That, I hoped, had its roots in the rock or rock solid roots.
But there's a breeze blowing, a stunning storm coming,
Thickening ink spills and swills on a bleating paper sky.
A crowd of rain on the horizon staggers nearer,
I sway so. I know so. I slip a little more.
I know so I sway so. I grip a little more.
These tender fingers in a clenched fist.
I must have slit my back. It hurts like a howl.
It stings like a scowl, weeps and stings again.
The skin splitting and spitting from my spine sides
And a pain develops muscles that create mouths
That simulate sounds of whole cities screaming.
There's a storm coming. A coming storm.
Dust spits from the clifftop into my river-eyes,
Forcing tears over the banks to flood me.
I will not drown in them. I will not drown.
I am hanging on. I am hanging on. I am hanging on.

In the zip of a thick ribbon of wind
A god or a devil appears floating in front of me
And tells me in a hunch of a NY accent
'Let go, let go – Death is just the beginning
Of the end of the beginning of the end . . . '
And continued for forty-one days and forty-one nights,
'Of the end of the beginning of the end . . . '
And in a crack of lightning the devil or the god vanished.
Nothing more to concentrate on. But a storm,
The sky. And my breaching back. And the cliff
And the edge. And the uprooting branch.
And my knuckles so sore, cracked and numb
They favour a knot of bleeding wood.
If I look down (and I do look down) I see

That blood has poured from my back; seeped
Along the smoothness of my backside; slid under
My testicles and coiled its way seductively
Around my thighs, knees and ebonised legs.
It pours in abundance from my feet and skydives.
I watch these red tears fall for ever and transform
Into explicit flowers as they reach the floor.
I will not become one. I am hanging on.
I am hanging on. I am hanging on.

Whispers from above me. From above me whispers gather
The cliff ledge lined with edgy people of all colours
Some humming 'Amazing Grace', others simply staring.
Some I saw pointing at my back and wincing.
A bearded man with his hand on a bible or a red book or a
    white book
Or a leather book or a revolutionary book or a dark green
    book
Shouted down to me in sermonic tones deeper than the sea,
'Let go. In the name of God. Let go!!'
A nervous follower peeps down and offers the advice that
'There's someone down there, they'll catch you.'
And before I get chance to answer they erupt into a sky
    shattering
'Someone's Crying, Lord – Let Go. Someone's Crying, Lord
    – Let Go.'
The harmony of those collected voices woke the spirit of the
    sky.

And they threw crosses at me. It's raining crosses.
I look down past my feet – a devil or a god
A man the size of a pea is mouthing the words 'Let go'.
Night-time was approaching. Breathless I whispered.
I will not fall. Never have. Never will. Not fall. Not fall.
But as quick as they came to help is as quick as they were
    gone.
But I am hanging on. I am hanging on. I am hanging on.

Darkness cloaked the horror of night-time,
Of gangrenous spirits that fed upon open wounds.
As lightning struck I saw glimpses of their faces;
Demons whose countenance had slipped;
Whose fingers had stretched and nails had curled;
Whose breath stank so viciously that I spewed to the sea
(My mantra: I am hanging on, I am hanging on, I am hanging
    on)
Throughout the darkness and fear until sunrise. And the
    stillness of

Morning breaking. I was a silhouette hanging from a branch
Against the chalky cliff. Only the sound of my trickling blood,
My breaking back and the moaning sky for comfort.
My shadow stretching across the cliff like a script title
On handmade paper.
The sulking storm retreated into the horizon to recollect –
Even the sea is trying to throw off its reflection.
I listened more, to the tearing of my back flesh as I hang,
The flapping wet skin of my bloodied back as it hangs
Tears painted salt veins along my ebonised skin.
As that stark sunlight skidded across a bloodied sky
I sensed the presence of two symmetrical shadows descending.
They stretched, seemingly even pushing back the clouds.
I felt them push warm air into my face.
I saw them in the corner of each eye. Magnificent wings
And felt the new muscles of my back and my chest expand
    with air.
Further and further. New air. New spirit. And there with not
    a soul around me
I unpeeled my tender fingers from that dew-drenched branch;
I let the sun pour into my eyes and finally after years I let go.
    Why?
Because I was growing. I was growing wings all the time. And
    I can fly.

LISTENER

Let There Be Peace

Let there be peace,
So frowns fly away like albatross
And skeletons foxtrot from cupboards;
So war correspondents become travel show presenters
And magpies bring back lost property,
Children, engagement rings, broken things.

Let there be peace,
So storms can go out to sea to be
Angry and return to me calm;
So the broken can rise and dance in the hospitals.
Let the aged Ethiopian man in the grey block of flats
Peer through his window and see Addis before him,
So his thrilled outstretched arms become frames
For his dreams.

Let there be peace.
Let tears evaporate to form clouds, cleanse themselves,
And fall into reservoirs of drinking water.
Let harsh memories burst into fireworks that melt
In the dark pupils of a child's eyes
And disappear like shoals of darting silver fish.
And let the waves reach the shore with a
Shhhhhhhhhh shhhhhhhhhh shhhhhhhhhh.

Rain

```
w  f  t  n  w  t  r  w  r  i  c
h  a  a  c  h  r  a  e  a  t  u
e  l  l  h  e  i  i  t  i  i  n
n  l  k  e  n  u  n  h  n  s  i
t  s  o  s  t  m  f  i  b  t  a
h  t  f  t  h  p  a  n  o  h  n
e  h  m  e  e  h  l  k  w  e  w
r  e  a  r     a  l  o  s  m  a
a  y     b     n  s  f     a  y
i        u     t           n
n        t
```

The Actor's Voice

This is a celebration of sound,
Of words said after the phone's put down,
After the door's shut at the editor's cut –
Of thoughts held after the word 'but . . . '
This is the sound. The actor's sound.
Of inflections after the flick of ash,
Before the crash, before the whiplash;
Of thoughts collecting before they arrive,
Of the deep breath before the dive.
This is the sound,
Of tender fingers in a clenched fist,
Of the wind carrying an invisible kiss,
Of a secret unfolding wish,
Before the candle blows like a lisp.

This is a celebration of sound,
Of words said after the phone's put down,
After the door's shut at the editor's cut –
Of thoughts said after the word 'but . . . '
Thoughts caught between the lines –
The reading sounds of needing minds.
This is the sound of beneath the laugh,
Beneath the draft, beneath the craft –
The space between the paragraphs.

Patterns

2. Have
7. Have
10. Innocence
5. Pattern
8. Lost
1. You
4. A
9. Your
3. Found
6. You

Laying the Table

We should prepare for arguments,
Lay down the tablecloth,
And silently place the cutlery
In exactly the right place.

We should serve each other's food
And eat with our hands,
Pick at the chicken,
Maul the potatoes.

We should then wipe our mouths
With the tablecloth and begin.

Perfect

You are so perfect
When you kick them the leaves flit to the trees,
Look back to you and applaud.
You are so perfect
Branches part in forests to share sunshine,
Squirrels watch you between acorns,
Foxes wake.

You are so perfect
Your winter coat buttons itself and hugs your heart,
Library books unfurl on tables, stretch
And wait for you to walk past.
Fast winter wind daren't touch you
But can't help brush your hair.

You are so perfect
Rivers have built their own bridges,
Knowing that one day you'll walk across them –
Just to catch your reflection they left a pile of stones for
    you to throw.
And the waves carry each stone to the bed, count them,
Look up at you and applaud.

You are so perfect
Traffic lights time themselves days before you arrive,
So your stride won't be broken and the cars can rest,
And the world can stop.
A table outside the café lays itself to the waiter's amazement,
Knowing that a man will stop for a coffee,
Knowing that you will walk past at 3.30 p.m.,
And he'd been waiting for you all of his life too.

Gambian Holiday Maker

        I

          Want

You

                To

Know

            How

          Stupid

You

    Sound

         When

You

    Talk

    To

      Us

         Like

This.

Listener

And if you were the evaporating tears
Then I would be the developing cloud.
There, the sound of rain,
The sound of the between-us sea,
The shingle shore gently fills our footsteps.
I have searched for you my entire life.
We have stood on opposite shores,
Listening to under-sea wails.
No translations as yet, but this.

I lie upon the earth-floor
As a lion might in deep dusk-sun.
Here I hear all the footsteps of the world
Reverberate in the beneath-me rocks,
Trying to find your first-person singular steps,
Trying to find a sentence in a history.
But the needle glints in the golden haystack
Of dawn; at the same time a strike of sunlight
Lances its eye. The world is smaller,
The larger my knowledge – still.

Standing, I hear the sun rise,
Not the birds of morning nor the cock crowing.
The cars coughing, the footsteps of early workers
Muffled in the red dust trudging through sleepless mystery,
But I hear the actual sun rising.

And as a sea can turn to dust before the eyes
I hear you through the sand storm – *the needle!*
Slow running from the red terror,
Arms wide to protect yourself or welcome me,
Feet dragging through sand and globules of blood,
Burning in the heatwave, wiping hot sand from your face,
Men with guns on the horizon far behind you,
The past tense threatening your presence.

I hear a concert of AK47s click, as thousands
Reload. The heat is tremendous – you have a radio.
But the sound of sand lifting from the ground
In the grip of the wind disturbs – you understand what is
    happening,
Not through sight but through the sounds.
I could almost hear you, your breathing
As you gave birth again, and another sister
Opened her eyes. Her wet face of sand.

In the drawing of this drama, the mist of mystery
Rising above the airwaves and heatwaves,
We have scattered around the world.
Revolutions between us. Implosions of conscience.
Corrupting earthquakes have split our family – between us
Swallows migrate above the Atlantic Ocean,
Pixellating the sky on tidal waves of heat
With such damnable ease.

Ricochet

A man shot a man who was a father,
The son of the dead father shot the father of the other son
Who was the man who had shot the first father.
Then I was born – I was told it didn't matter,
'Cause time had passed.

But my uncle who was holding the pain
Of his dead brother – who was my father –
Said he couldn't forgive because every year,
Every minute of every day, he loved his brother,
And consequently there was a score to settle.

I am living here because there was a revolution,
And some say this was why the man killed the father in
The first place – our family lost our property.
But I can go back – I am a man now.

The son of the neighbour who was the original killer
Was living in our house at home, said that he owned it now.
My uncle travelled back, to our homeland, but no longer,
No longer felt at home in his own homeland. He took a gun,
Which was owned by an old friend of the counter-revolution,
And shot himself. And the neighbour who was the son of
The man who I was told was a killer told me, at his funeral,
That his dad hadn't shot first – that my dad had.

Email

I shall be totally honest with you
And mean all that I say. *Delete Undo.*
Without you I am incomplete,
Less of the man I know I am. *Delete.*
Less your heart, mine won't beat but burn.
Delete Delete Delete Return.

Elephant in the Room

It isn't what's said, it's what's not said
What says it all.
The day you brought it home
I'll never forget.
It was only seven foot tall then.
An elephant! I said.
Put it in the backyard.
Fine, you said, *Fine!*
And, disgruntled,
Tied it to the washing line.

As you slept I'd pull back the curtains,
Stand by the window and watch it.
A dark shadow. An iceberg. A hump filled the backyard,
Rising and falling with each deep gentle snore.

Breakfasts were never the same again.
The elephant took up all the space
And had no table manners whatsoever,
Although it was useful for the washing-up.
Whenever I broached the subject,
You'd rant and rave and fume,
Say I was going crazy, *There is no elephant in the room.*

But the saddest thing is not the crockery it smashed
Nor the walls it demolished, of our past.
It wasn't its footsteps stamped all over our home,
The cracked floorboards or its wont to roam.
It was the lie established after I said, *It's there.*
For years you looked at me and said, *Where, dear, where?*

Architecture

Each cloud wants to be a storm.
My tap water wants to be a river.
Each match wants to be an explosive.
Each reflection wants to be real.
Each joker wants to be a comedian.
Each breeze wants to be a hurricane.
Each drizzled rain wants to be torrential.
Each laugh from the throat wants to burst from the belly.
Each yawn wants to hug the sky.
Each kiss wants to penetrate.
Each handshake wants to be a warm embrace.
Don't you see how close we are to crashes and confusion,
Tempests and terror, mayhem and madness,
And all things out of control?

Each melting ice cube wants to be a glacier.
Each goodbye wants to be the smooth stroke of a forehead.
Each cry wants to be a scream.
Each carefully pressed suit wants to be creased.
Each midnight frost wants to be a snow drift.
Each mother wants to be a friend.
Each night-time wants to strangle the day.
Each wave wants to be tidal.
Each subtext wants to be a title.
Each winter wants to be the big freeze.
Each summer wants to be a drought.
Each polite disagreement wants to be a vicious denial.
Each diplomatic smile wants to be a one-fingered tribute
To tact.
Don't you see how close we are to crashes and confusion,
Tempests and terror, mayhem and madness,
And all things out of control?

                              Keep telling yourself,
                              You've got it covered.

Moving Mountains

I climbed a mountain for her,
Then saw a frown upon her.
She said I only climbed up here,
So I could look back down on her.

Manchester Piccadilly

These eyes are the windows to my soul,
Before them Piccadilly dreams unfold.
This city of freedom, of future, of fame.
I catch a dream, catch a pathway, a plane,
I got Piccadilly mapped upon my skin.
I got her reflection shining out from within.
I got my coffee to go in the place I stay.
I got what's coming tomorrow, today.

I got all that I need here in the palm of my hand.
Every time Piccadilly grows, I expand.
Reflected in these windows, the eyes to my soul,
The discovery, the cave of gold.
I got Piccadilly in my heart, in my veins.
I get high from her hope, from her name,
From the mirrored buildings that scrape the sky.
I got the hard sell and the good buy.

I got it all here. I got it all at my fingertips.
I let the words flower from my tongue's tip.
I got this city mapped into my skin.
I take it all easy but I take it all in.
I got these pathways, these patterns within.
I take it all easy. I take it all in.
I hear the sound of hope, its truest tone.
I got Piccadilly. I got the city. I got home.

I got this A to Z in my head. It's like I said,
Here are my waking dreams, my bed.
I got these reflections of outside, within,
I take it all easy. I take it all in.
I got these designs inside my mind,
I got the power of reason, of the line,
I got all that I need here in the palm of my hand.
Every time Piccadilly grows, I expand.

Some Things I Like

(A poem to shout)

I like wrecks, I like ex-junkies,
I like flunks and ex-flunkies,
I like the way the career-less career,
I like flat beer,
I like people who tell half stories and forget the rest,
I like people who make doodles in important written tests,
I like being late. I like fate. I like the way teeth grate,
I like laceless shoes, chordless blues,
I like the one-bar blues,
I like buttonless coats and leaky boats,
I like rubbish tips and bitten lips,
I like yesterday's toast,
I like cold tea, I like reality,
I like ashtrays, I write and like crap plays.

I like curtains that don't quite shut,
I like bread knives that don't quite cut,
I like rips in blue jeans,
I like people who can't say what they mean,
I like spiders with no legs, pencils with no lead,
Ants with no heads, worms that are half dead.
I like holes, I like coffee cold. I like creases in neat folds.
I like signs that just don't know where they're going,
I like angry poems,
I like the way you can't pin down the sea.
See.

**** This

**** this, **** all that
Who the **** are you shouting at?
**** you and what you're shouting for
**** you all, I don't care no more
**** it, you are the dead loss
**** you and **** your ****ing boss
Not much to say, no ****er to tell
**** **** **** it **** in' hell.

Magpie

I saw a single magpie,
It really got to my head.
I thought, 'You unlucky bastard,'
And shot the bugger dead.

Before We Get Into This

Before we get to know each other
And sing for tomorrow
And unearth yesterday,
So that we can prepare our joint grave,
You should know that I have no family,
Neither disowned nor distanced – none.

No birthdays, nor Christmas,
No telephone calls. It's been that way
Since birth, for what it's worth,
No next of skin.

I am the guilty secret of an innocent woman
And a dead man – tell your parents, they'll want to know.

Advice for the Living

Dead fast this.
Everyone's dying to arrive,
Living for deadlines, trying to
Stay straight as a die. They'll get
There, dead or alive because they're
Dead set, and they do arrive in shores
Of dead heats, dead beats at dead ends
Dead messed up like dead stock. The living
Dead flogging dead horses in the dead of
Night. Dead right, dead lost, dead right.
Every now and again we stop dead
In our tracks, dead still 'cause it's
Dead hard, like a dead weight's
Dropped on the head. . .Wouldn't
You die for a little piece, die for
A breath of hope? Dead right,
I would. In the dead centre of
All this deadlocking, dread
Locked. Words, dead ahead.
They read: *Life is not worth*
living if there's no one you
would die for. Dead right.

The Battle of Adwa, 1896

Preceding Adwa

Remember this, the Europeans
Carved up our homes with blood thirst,
Not because we were the Third World,
But because we were the First.
Because we held gold in our hearts,
Because we had diamonds for eyes,
Because oil ran through our veins,
And a blessing hung in our skies.

Remember this, that when they scrambled
In the conference in Berlin
And callously carved Africa,
Searing each African's skin,
It was not just because of their greed
Or need to sow seeds saturated with sorrow,
But because through Africa's greatness
They envisioned their own great tomorrow.

The Beginning

Baratieri, the Italian general, had ice instead of eyes
And a tongue of five leather whips.
Ras Alula was deafened by the whisper
Of lies that seeped from his lips.
Through Alula's agents who could read
The tone of Ethiopian winds,
Their whisper, *We will catch the Italian advance*
Before the advance begins.
And with anger, that of lions,
And a swiftness of eagles' wings,
Alula rose magnificent and rode
To the foot of Menelik the king;

With all their five generals, Menelik growled,
Five armies and damned attacks,
It will take one strong Ethiopia
To break their stiffened backs.

Meantime, with pomp and primitive greed,
The Italians embarked upon their plan;
They left for Adwa from Entisco
With night-time a shroud for each man.
Unbeknown every step was recorded
By Alula's silent speedy spies
Who traced the battalion's movement
Through the reflections they left in the sky.
The Italians noting the Ethiopian dawn
As a cloak for the surprise attack
Had no knowledge that warriors were waiting
And would give the surprise back.
With all their five generals, Ras Alula whispered,
Their armies and planned attacks,
It will take one strong Ethiopia
To break their brittle backs.

The War

The Ethiopians advanced from below,
A hero's sacrifice for a country's love
Suffice as they fell and blood spilled
For another flank to rein from above,
And so unveiled complex manoeuvres
Of hope and honour for history
Whose aim the breaking of evil
And the waking of victory.
The Ethiopians from all provinces
Gathered with truth as protection
Descended around Adwa with justice and honour
And unity as their weapon.
The cracking snapping of rattling rifles

Awoke the morning sun;
From ridges the Italians poured fire
The Battle of Adwa begun:

With all their five generals Ras Mengesha fought,
With their armies and their attacks.
It will take one strong Ethiopia
To snap their stiffened backs.

The Victory

It seemed the more Ethiopians were killed
The more returned.
The more they tried to drench their spirits
The more the spirits burned.
It seemed as if amongst the red mist
Each man who fell wounded rose again,
Each breath of air rejuvenated his lungs,
Each drop of blood seeped back to his veins.
It seemed that the Ethiopians
Rose from the river beds,
Came from the shadows of mountainsides,
With eyes of stone and dread,
And Baratieri's generals, sensing
The beginning of the end,
Succumbed to the deafening whisper,
Surrender, surrender.

Remember this: it was not one of Ethiopia,
But Ethiopia as one;
It was not part of the sum that won,
But part of everyone.
It was not the heart on its own,
But its veins that pumped on.

It was not just the warriors,
But where they were all from.

Remember this: how the story washed
Across the continent enslaved,
Flooded with the story of Adwa
In a whispered tidal wave,
From Kenya to Senegal,
From Morocco to the Gambia.
The liberation began in Adwa, 1896,
And ended in South Africa.

The Gilt of Cain

Here is the *ask price* on the *closed position*,
History is no inherent acquisition.
For here the *technical correction* upon the act,
A *merger* of truth and in *actuals* fact,
On the *spot*, on the money – the *spread*.
The *dealer* lied when the *dealer* said,
The *bull* was charging, the *bear* was dead,
The market must calculate *per capita*, not head.

And great traders *acting in concert*, arms rise,
As the *actuals* fraught on the sea of *franchise*
Thrown overboard into the *exchange* to drown
In distressed *brokers'* disconsolate frown.
In *accounting liquidity* is a mounting morbidity
But raising the arms with such rigid rapidity . . .
Oh, the reaping, the raping rapacious *fluidity*,
The violence, the vicious and vexed *volatility*.

The roaring trade floor rises above crashing waves:
The traders buy ships, beneath the slaves.
Sway machete back, sway machete again,
Crick crack *cut back* the Sugar Rush, Cain.
The *whipsaw*, it's all, and the whip saw it all,
The *rising market* and the cargo fall.
Who'll enter 'Jerusalem', make the *margin call* for Abel?
Who will kick over the stall and turn the table?

Cain gathers cane as *gilt*-gift to his land,
But whose sword of truth shall not sleep in hand?
Who shall unlock the *stocks and share*,
Break the *bond*, the bind unbound – lay bare
The truth? *Cash flow* runs deep but spirit deeper,
You ask the question, 'Am I my brother's keeper?'
I answer the best way *I* can, through laws.
My name, my brother, Wilberforce.

Applecart Art

Upset the art, smash the applecart,
Sell it for firewood to warm hearts.
Don't join the loop, the loop troupe,
Don't hump through their hoops,
Or get stuck on sticky peaks of double speak.
I'm clocking the click of the clique.
I swim with the shallow.
If they demand I be deep,
Though, I can hold my breath
Deeper than sleep, deeper than death.

Upset the art, crash the snapplecart,
Sell it for cash and a brand new start.
Turn cart wheels on the art wheels,
If that's how your heart feels.
To those who demand you stand by their pandect,
Call them all cheats on call and collect,
They're gargoyles hunched on their haunches,
Stalking the walk at lunches and launches.
They backbite, backslap, salubriously clap,
With cleaver hands to stick in the back.

Upset the art, trash the cattlecart,
Start the stampede in the heart of the art.
Don't play poker with the mediocre,

Token-filled pack full of jokers.
The Class A offenders are pretenders
Protecting their pretence, return them to sender.

Feel fierce flocks of fight forming and flowing,
Know you're only as good as your last poem.
Cut yourself, it should be ink you're bleeding,
Know you're only as good as your last reading.
Let wisdom be the weight of your wealth
And your greatest competitor, yourself.

I Will Not Speak Ill of the Dead

In the orchard I catch a falling leaf and wish to make no wish.
Before my eyes the leaf, a veined slither of heart, pulsates.
A collar-boned branch snaps beneath or behind or within,
But I am here for a reason and cannot wait to leave.

I won't speak ill of the dead.
Not a word as I reach, twist, then with a tug of the wrist
Pick the scarlet fruit from the bitter memory tree.
The sound of a hiss pours down in a shiver and circles me.
This is not fruit for eating. This bulbous leathery bruised
Over-sized bull's eye, a cross between a lychee and an apple,
Seeps sticky brown oil that coils into my half-formed fist.

I am told this flesh is poisonous and so it is my service
That I should bring it to my mouth beneath my nose,
Smell and draw the decaying cancerous tinge.
Slow but deliberate, I sink my teeth into its stringy slime
And feel the cold flesh slide up my teeth and onto my gums.
The first bite is the worst bite and the brown oil slides
Down my chin as the mulch slips within me.

This is good. I am impervious to the poison, because
I was fed the seeds of this tree when I slept as a child.
It grows inside me. I feel its branches stretch inside
And at night-time sometimes I hear it tear my inner flesh.

Though a hand has become one deformed knot,
The other holds a wooden pen.

I won't *speak* ill of the dead. Not a word.
There will be nothing more satisfying than knowing that
The sewage with all its pips and dangerous seeds
Will be dragged away from me, spat out into the sea
A long way away – I will not speak ill of the dead.
Not a word.

Transistor

Airwaves transmit, vocals translate,
Emotions in transit transmigrate,
Story transmutes and what transpires
Are transfinite transonic choirs.
The soldier, the teacher, the lover, the storm,
Translocate, transform.

This Train (Sing Along)

This train is bound for Wigan, this train.
This train is bound for Wigan, this train.
This train is bound for Wigan.
Praise the lord 'cause it's a big 'un.
This train is bound for Wigan, this train.

Spring: Mayday Mayday

I can always tell when it's spring. There's this plane crash,
And it happens to crash into our house.
It's as sure a sign as any sign is.
I step into the kitchen and there it is: the wreckage.
Thick girders of light split the house from every direction.
Half the plane's fuselage is in the sink, soaked in hot oil,
Tick tick ticking – the sound of sulking metal cooling.
There's glass everywhere.

The pilot seat has stuck in the boiler. Again.
And a fountain of steam sprays bouquets of hissing greys.
A map in the corner tries to hide from the horror,
Its wet roads have spilled into rivers that have spilled into
     towns
That have fallen down the sides of valleys.
Postcards like doves flit through thick dusted light.
There's burst suitcases everywhere. Everywhere.
A sign stuck in the larder door reads 'Emergency Exit'.

I look up at the ceiling, the rotator blades have crashed
     through,
Drunkenly swirling oily smoke coils through the blue.
A tannoy sprawled on the washing machine, its neck snapped,
Wails to the floor where the cracked control panel is,
Where a mangle of oxygen feeder wires hiss their last breath.
The wing tips in the front room in the television screen,
Its red flashing light bleeding, the room ticks selfishly.

And the curtains are blowing outside on a fractured windowsill.
The landing gear's in the garden, in the laburnum tree,
Its wheels still spinning. Doesn't even know it's landed.
Secrets and lies all over the place. Half-written postcards.
The emergency crews won't come. They say there's
'Too much radiation. There's too much friction.'

'It's all too dangerous,' they say. 'And anyway
A little spring cleaning'll sort it all out.'

So here I am,
As the laburnum tree twists its yellow fingers
Around broken pieces of plane; it's that time of year again.
I can smell it in the rain. It's the time of year to clean it all up;
      It's the time of year for the crash and the time of year
         to tidy it up;
To find new places to put the wreckage, to make ornaments
  maybe,
     To find new places for burst luggage, to sew it up maybe,
Give it away, maybe. It's time to dig holes in the garden.

To bury it!
Time of year to cover it all and grow new plants.
Until next year when the strange fruit bursts from the earth,
Triumphant as afterlife, and falls from the skies, as if *real*.
That's how I know it's spring. See. See.
I woke this morning to find the garden and my home a wreck.
Pieces of plane. Gnarled metal, glinting with dew,
And sunrise painting the whole scene a metallic red.
It's spring again.

Barley Field

The barley field wished but swayed,
Washed by rain, dried by the sun,
And combed by the wind.

The Oak stands, centre page,
I feel her stretch as morning pushes back the sheets.
Her leaves twist in the breeze like the hands
Of Indian dancers, and the sun shoots through them,
Making shoals of golden fish swim through her shadow.

I was looking for inspiration, and there it was.
Not in the field nor the sun nor the Oak,
Barely visible NG+DA – in the trunk.
I had been here before. The memory flooded,
And there I was in that sea of barley,
Barely seeing you.

The Boxer

(*For Phil Martin 1955–1994*)

He saw riots scream and the blue sky scream
In the memory in smoke that lingered.
He saw furrowed frowns and nervous breakdowns
And outsiders who pointed their fingers.
They painted it blue and believed the news
That barks about the violence and crime.
He saw them scuttle like roaches, past him in coaches,
Their Moss Side is in their mind.

A boxer by trade and never afraid
Of the fingers that point at his home,
He built from foundations, made a soul nation,
A palace grew from the stones.
He made princes kings, lords of the ring,
Made them swing like ballerinas on glass.
He taught inner strength and discipline,
Peace and the power to last.

Governments came having heard the name
Of the man who built champions and dreams,
Who against all the odds with his will and God's
Got to the top with the crop and the cream.
He made rights from wrong, made the weak strong,
Gave hope where it seemed there was none.
His legacy stands and lives on in this land;
The Champ, the man, has gone.

Torch

One day you may find
That all is not dictated by time;
That a river is rushing through your head,
Or a stampede of black doves from your eyes.

One day you may find that the ground
Which you once crawled on, learned to walk on, is sinking,
And the air that you drink in is hot,
And there are no cul-de-sacs, just motorways with no signs,
Horizons with no hills or trees.

One day you may find that your small world
Is no longer so small
But a space too big to take in.
Out of your mind friends say hello,
You are two minutes behind,
And by the time they think you're a little weird, it's too late.
The letters you receive in the post
Are from the ghost of yourself,
And you reflect on the defects and in effect
You are rejecting all that you ever were.

One day you may look in the mirror
And see into yourself.
All the tubes, holes and rushing hormones
Fighting each other for air with swords.
And one day you may bring yourself to yourself
And fight yourself until your soul lies
Like dead roses.

One day you may kick the shit out of yourself,
To get out of the shit you've become.
One day you may face your mirror, falter in shock,
At what's looking back at you,
'Cause that's not you!

One day you may fall on the floor,
'Cause the shit you are in has grown claws
And is gripping your neck.
You're a shipwrecked defect
Looking for a place to hide.

NEW POEMS

What If

A lost number in the equation,
A simple, understandable miscalculation.
And what if on the basis of that
The world as we know it changed its matter of fact.

Let me get it right. What if we got it wrong?
What if we weakened ourselves getting strong?
What if we found in the ground a vial of proof?
What if the foundations missed a vital truth?

What if the industrial dream sold us out from within?
What if our impenetrable defence sealed us in?
What if our wanting more was making less?
And what if all of this . . . it wasn't progress?

Let me get it right. What if we got it wrong?
What if we weakened ourselves getting strong?
What if our wanting more was making less?
And what if all of this wasn't progress?

What if the disappearing rivers of Eritrea,
Were the rising tide of encroaching fear?
What if the tear inside the protective skin
Of Earth was trying to tell us something?

Let me get it right. What if we got it wrong?
What if we weakened ourselves getting strong?
What if the message carried in the wind
Was saying something?

From butterfly wings to the hurricane,
It's the small things that make great change
In the question towards the end of the leases,
No longer the origin but the end of species.

LIVERPOOL JOHN MOORES UNIVERSITY
LEARNING SERVICES

Let me get it right. What if we got it wrong?
What if we weakened ourselves getting strong?
What if the message carried in the wind
Was saying something?

Whale Translation

I speak to you on this memorable day
Through the translation services of a poet.
I must commend Captain Boomer and his dedicated crew
On the good ships *Mercedes* and *Miss Daisy*,
Who thrashed through my seas to try and dissuade me,
And whose shadows traced me down the Thames to my end.
They are good men, good women,
But I did not want to be saved.

Do not be distressed at the sight of me, I am not lost.
I am a Messenger sent by I-Pod, the Ruling Council of Whales
And the Ministry of Oceans and Seas to the people of landmass,
Of Greenwich of London of Britain.
We have been trying to communicate with you for so long . . .
In New Zealand some years ago forty-six women and thirteen
    men
 – whales to you – crawled onto the beach and drowned in
    your air.
They were my family . . . my family.

I volunteered for this final voyage to meet them again
By the magnetic moon to the neap tide of the Thames,
Onto your single shingle shore among broken clay pipes,
    oyster shells,
And worry stones left by fine spring tides.
I have given my life on the cross harbour into the darkened
Mud chute onto the Island gardens of next life
Where I shall meet them again.
We are dark angels navigating the gravitational pull of solar
    and lunar.
I have a message . . .

You live in one per cent of your thirty per cent of Earth.
Our oceans cover seventy per cent. It is ours. It is yours.
The whale nation knows all your migrations.

We felt the scour of wind rush upon our sea as she surged
From the Caribbean in 1948 and landed in Tilbury on June
    22nd.
We felt the trembling footsteps through the great partition of
Landmass of what was, is now, India and Pakistan.

We were rippled by shadows of slave ships, in the Age of Sail,
They whipped the oceans back and cut the skin of sea with cat
    o' nine tails,
And we saw those Africans float before us like
Shoals of black squid squirting ink in plumes.
Four hundred years later we felt the tremor of great migration
Of free African slaves from the Deep South to the North.
There is climate change.
Now we feel the down pressure of air as each plane crosses the
    Channel
Bringing great Polish men and women to these shores.
We feel this in our seas: this is why I was sent by the Ruling
    Council of Whales
And the Ministry of Oceans and Seas.

Birth is migration from the womb to the open air.
We are all immigrants.
Death is migration of breath and air,
The last migration, the vast migration.
Migration is our nature,
I have been sent to tell you.
Echo location. Echo location.

The Spark Catchers

Tide twists on the Thames and lifts the lea to the brim of Bow
There, shoals of sirens work by way of the waves
At the fire factory, the fortress of flames.

In tidal shifts East London Lampades made
Millions of matches that lit candles for the well-to-do
And the ne'er-do-well to do alike. Strike.

The greatest threat to their lives was
The sulphurous spite-filled spit of diabolo,
The molten madness of a spark.

They became spark catchers, and on the word 'strike'
A parched arched woman would dive
With hand outstretched to catch the light.

And land like a crouching tiger with fist high,
Holding the malevolent flare tight,
Till it became an ash dot in the palm.

The women applauded the magnificent grace,
The skill it took, the mid-air pirouette,
The precision, perfection and peace.

Beneath stars by the bending bridge of Bow,
In the silver sheen of a phosphorous moon,
They practised Spark Catching.
'The fist, the earth, the spark, its core
The fist, the body, the spark, its heart'
The Matchgirls march.

Lampades, the torch bearers,
The catchers of light.
Sparks fly. Matchgirls strike.

Shipping Good

The clock clicks in a child's hand
As she skips to the ticks and tocks.
Under the park tunnels run from the dark
While sun circles the clocks.

Flowers grow for those that know
To bloom is to know your roots,
To give the earth all it's worth,
Tend to the new shoots.

And a horse on course its hooves
Drum beneath the earth
Where dreadnoughts' sleeping seamen
Are weeping for the berth.

While the marshes sigh at night,
When sky dives into the Thames,
Greenwich and I will sleep again
And wake again as friends.

It is the thudding in my ear
Upon the pillow that sounds
As a black mare churning
Dreams from the ground.

As she charges towards
The Meridian Line,
Leaps Shepherd's Gate,
And dives into time.

Where an ancient mariner
His guest no longer cross,
Sings songs of his wrongs
To a circling albatross.

A coffee cup lifts to the face,
In its reflection a woman sees the sea
Where a small girl in a boat smiles.
She whispers, '*This must be me.*'

And the girl cranes her neck,
She sails the swirls in the cup
And smiles for a minute and frowns
And holds the flowers up.

Here lies the beginning of time,
Where the river cradles the land,
Here lies the roundabout,
About the sun and the sand.

And the star rises on Observatory Hill
And watches them watching him,
And the water spills on a quiet wharf
Where the silver mermaids swim.

And a woman collects the crests
And takes them home to spin,
She makes sails for the high road
For our dreams to begin.

Open Up

Where did all that cotton come from
That filled the employment factories the mills?
Why do you think Indians came here and Africans
With their calm and their sense and their skills?

Nobody owes anybody anything in this world,
But all this world is for all and every one.
And borders are bullies and boring,
So let's have done with them. Let's get them gone.

Let's have no north and no south,
Only truth and lies.
And let's see how we understand the world then,
Find out where lies the land and the land ties.

I'm from north western tribe.
We say good morning, we drink tea.
We walk to Rivington Pike each year,
From Atherton, Bolton, and Leigh.

But more than any other point
In its growth and self-improving,
I can tell the confidence of any street
When a stranger moves in.

The more closed we become,
The more foreign our spirits seem,
The more closed we become,
The more our heart's quarantined.

The more closed we become,
The darker our heart,
The more closed we become,
The more apart.

The more territorial,
More terrorist.

Open all borders, break down all walls.
Shred all birth certificates, burn all passports.
Open all doors, windows and gates.
Open all access-all areas, open all records.

Open all fields, open all curtains.
Open all memories, open all galleries.
Open all fears, open all dreams, open all.
Cure all maladies.

Open all educational facilities.
Open all secret services, open all doors.
Open all senses, open all defences.
Ask what were these closed for.

Open all family secrets, open all trap doors.
Open all dark passages, open all attics and cellars.
Open all battles, open all secret wars.
Open all, and unlock interstella . . . The interstella.

The possibilities of light.
The nature of trust.
The strength of the unassailable
US.

Night Mails

This is the night mail crossing the border,
And oblige, bark the bailiffs, by order,
Letters from providence, letters to the poor,
The lot on the corner, the girl next door.
Pulling out tears on debt's steady climb,
The grades are against her on poverty's line.
She carries the past like it were a boulder,
Shovelling screams over her shoulder,
Snorting noisily as law passes,
The children like wind bent grasses.
Some turn heads as invisibility approaches,
She stares on the sideline at blank-faced coaches.
Seems no one can turn her course,
As she stumbles, broken by unspoken laws.
In disquiet she passes yet no one wakes,
And shoulders in bedrooms gently shake.

Dawn does not freshen, her climb is undone.
Down towards depression she descends,
Towards thugs yelping in shades of shame,
Towards fields of statistics and furnaces.
Set upon the dark plain, like giant chessmen,
Her family waits for her.
In the dark of them, beside pale steel locks
Men long for news.

No letters of thanks, nor from the banks,
No letters of joy from the girl or the boy,
(But receipted bills and citations
to inspect new stock or their relations),
Nor applications for situations,
No letters above declarations,
Of her illegality and complications,
And gossip, gossip, plans for nations,
News substantial, no ring-fenced financials.

Letters with faces scrawled in the margin,
The breakdown uploads, the bailiffs charge in,
No letters from uncle, cousins nor aunt –
They too locked in the same dance.

Letters of demand delivered by hand,
Letters of law delivered by claw,
Written on paper of every hue,
I think the violence is fighting you;
The cold and official pouring,
Into the breaking passage of falling.
Clever, stupid, short and the long,
The typed replies spelled all wrong.

Thousands are still asleep,
Dreaming of increasing demands,
Of disappearing in the quicksand,
Or invisibility like Branston's and Crawford's.
But we shall continue our dreams,
Shall wake soon and long for letters,
And no one will hear the postman's knock
Without a quickening of the heart,
For who can bear themselves forgotten?

Lock and Quay

The moon is a scuffle hunter scouring the sky
For what might be left of the sun; meantime

Light horsemen pave the way for day-plunderers
To take the game ship and steal wonders.

Mudlarks wait in sludge for lumpers to throw
Goods off the ship. Into outstretched hands of night

Shift work shifts on shifty shifting tides.
Not even Pepys knew of the gilt silt tythe

That slipped past him in black straps or Jemmy,
In shadow of admiralty and cross-silvered palms.

In this cargo of words the wards of memory quay,
The Game Lightmen and dockers, the workers

Of wave, wind and wharf,
The watermen, the tag rag and bobtail poor

Whose names long forgotten by all accounts,
Whose ghostly barges slide across celestial seas

Are now ancient mariners that carry tales
Of nature's people in the age of sail.

To these contours of lock and quay and made ground
Open the coffer dam via the green cut.

Where watercourse was is where you are
This poem is the balance beam. Gongoozlers

Let go. Once a canal from river through earth
Now walk on the pastures of water.

Underneath footnotes the past sleeps
Footsteps like thunder ripple deep.

These words unearthed and cut by hand
Hewn from the past. This promised land.

Beneath sky and earth lock and quay
This stone holds them in memory.

The workers of now, the workers of then,
The unnamed women the unnamed men.

Look through the metropolitan sway
In the swilling light the swirling day.

Ghost boats slide past at night
Like clouds in morning sunlight.

Listening Post

Here are the past messages of the first born,
The last words of the front,
The first waves of spring tides,
Where night bathes the sun.

Here are the words of letters unwritten,
The tongue tied and unread,
The hymns of the uncongregated,
The unheard song unsaid.

Water, tears weightless for years,
Rise upwards from fallen eyes.
Here are the swallows returning,
The crops lifting the sky.

Here is the blood, the blood dread sun,
Climbing the edge of plight.
She holds in hands the power to stun
All darkness stilled in the night.

Slow shadows stretch and slant,
Seeds split beneath earth.
Roots of light seek the eye,
The opening irises at birth.

And here is the child born,
The harvest in bloom.
My hands hold him to light,
To dawn and the falling moon.

Light paves the way,
Night waves reveal,
The breaking new day,
Above dew-soaked fields.

We cannot be defined by war,
Not by fields sown with sorrow,
Not by the death that befell you all,
But by the peace that followed.

Look what has risen from the fallen
Above long shadows cast.
The light that shines on open minds,
The torch held in our past.

If you could hear at the listening post
One hundred years ahead,
And be, as you are, the missing host
Where light and darkness wed . . .

Look what was sown by the stars,
At night, across the fields.
We are not defined by scars at all,
But by the incredible ability to heal.

Here are the past messages of the first born,
The last words of the front,
The first waves of spring tides,
Where night bathes the sun.

Fallen

The bridge between girl and woman,
Between found and lost,
Between caught and fallen,
Between faith and frost.

She may turn to salt
Should her head turn.
The guilt like silt, the fault,
Burn, burn and burn.

That mother falls from daughter
And flies from the ridge,
That this is thicker than water
Which runs under the bridge.

That swells by the banks
And fights immovable rocks,
That spills over ledges
In the rapids of unwashed.

I am your son!
And you did not fall,
And I did not fall from you
At all: not at all.

I came from those rivers.
You floated amongst reeds.
I rise from the fallen,
The swollen seed.

Let go. They said, let go.
Unworthy unwashed,
The discordant lullaby,
What lament of loss.

They may have burned
The birth ribbon,
But of all things I have learned
You are forgiven.
You are not to blame,
Not the carrier of gifts,
Not the winged flame,
Famed heroine of myth.

Bring me Artemis with her hounds,
And Antigone with soil in her hair,
Bring me Athena and Boudica alive,
Bring Jane Eyre.

Bring me Gaea, the daughter of chaos,
Bring me Daphne and her olive roots,
Bring me Lisbeth Salander,
The girl with the dragon tattoo.

Bring me Ursula of the oceans,
Helen and her thousand ships,
Bring Sethe and Fevvers,
And Medusa with blood on her lips.

Bring me Eve, bring Ruth,
Bring me Mary after the birth,
Bring back Medeba on her chariot,
Bring Rhea, goddess of earth.

Bring me Pandora with hope,
Bring me fierce Delilah,
Bring me Persephone in spring,
Bring the Queen of Sheba.

And tell *them* of the fallen,
Of the bad blooded women,
Of the unwashed unbelievers,
The unforgiven.

Though I am the son of sullen,
I have found my calling.
They say you fell from grace,
But you were never fallen.

Simply on the bridge between girl and woman,
Between found and lost,
Between caught and fallen,
Between faith and frost.

Belong

Have you seen the churches of Lalibela?
Swum in the warm springs of Addis Ababa?
Have you heard the reaching Nile
Of the bible and the Koran, my Abyssinia?

Have you heard whispering widow peaks of sand?
Seen the reeling rainbows as Victoria falls?
Felt the mists on the Simien mountains
And the dust clouds of Harare's hyenas call?

And did you see the gentle man taken,
Then imprisoned for twenty-five years,
Who walked out of chains and became president,
And who faced down the world's fears?

Did you see his example to the world,
How he embraced his adversary,
Spoke of unassailable truth and reconciliation?
Then we flounder in wars' anniversaries.

Hold me while spirits of the past
And rivers of blood run through me.
All this past feeds this present
And brings the truth into me.

His story, your search, his journey ours,
Something rings true inside and strong.
I stand atop Piccadilly Tower and sing,
I belong, I belong.

I, the Mogadishan who knows troubled waters.
I, the Belfast man who knows troubled cities.
I, the Ethiopian who knows troubled lands.
I, the Serbian who crosses troubled seas.

Who walked through darkened valleys
Under the shadows of death and bled,
And who lay amongst the freshly killed
And in fear of tears played dead.

Those who have cried cities, sobbed roads,
In the name of here and where they came from,
Stand with children atop Bridgewater Hall
And sing, I belong here, I belong.

I am the blackest blackest blackest man,
The tongue twists the skin dark.
I moved next door to the whitest poet
In John Cooper Clarke.

I'm buried in the cemetery where Morrissey walked,
In the earth from where grew Stone Roses.
I am the seamstress for Manchester's dream coat,
I designed the clothes for Moses.

I am the PSV, the sanctuary, the kitchen.
I am the reno red rhythm, the Bull Ring's blues.
I am the dread in its red, and for all that's said,
Wherever I go I am you.

I grew in the villages of Lancashire.
You stood on my horizon since birth.
The reason I came to Manchester
Is because it's the greatest place on earth.

I bring my past, I bring my future,
I bring my rights and I bring my song.
I stand atop the Hacienda and shout,
We belong here, we belong.

Rest

(*For Carol Ann Duffy*)

I expect you might at some point tonight
Beneath the sheets before sleep,
Still reeling from the flaying lights,
Want or more likely seek

Rest. There is no manifesto in this,
Nor snake-like list of things to do.
There is no tomorrow, either.
There's poetry, as ever, and you.

Adventure Flight

Third planet from the sun, this spinning earth.
Thousands of football cups but only one is first.
Here comes the light to break the pitch: the new day.
Crowds wake! Clouds break! The adventure is under way.

I will not waiver. I will not fall. I will not cower.
When under great pressure the great overpower.
We are equal in dreams – underdogs and over achievers.
We are nothing without adventures and believers.

There's everything to gain: everything to prove.
Touch and be touched, move and be moved.
Summon all resources, steal chance, take risk.
The challenge, the adventure, the grit.

One game, one destiny, one goal, one curved ball of Earth.
One and all, young and old, more than gold is worth.
All four corners, this field this cup – our number one –
When against all odds carry on, shout, 'Carry on.'

Make wings of your arms with the heart. At its centre
The challenge, the flight, the adventure.

Endnotes

'Whale Translation'

In 2013 a giant sperm whale was found on the beach in Greenwich and became national news. This super-real art installation is the work of the Belgian arts collective Captain Boomer, created in collaboration with Zephyr Wildlife Reconstruction. I was artist in residence at the Greenwich and Docklands International Festival.

'The Spark Catchers'

'The Spark Catchers' is the first poem commissioned for the 2012 London Olympics. The poem remains in the Olympic Park as a Landmark poem and will do so for the next hundred years.

'Shipping Good'

'Shipping Good' was commissioned in 2012 by the Cathedral Group. It is a Landmark Poem and can be found in the new developments outside Greenwich Station.

'Open Up' and 'Belong'

'Open Up' and 'Belong' are commissions by Manchester Literature Festival as a response to the fiftieth anniversary of Martin Luther King's era-defining 'I have a dream' speech for a celebratory programme co-produced with Manchester Camerata. It was performed at Manchester Town Hall on Saturday, 19 October 2013, interspersed between movements of Beethoven's String Quartet No. 13 in B flat, OP. 130, played by Camerata's principal players.

'Night Mails'

In the café in the Midland Hotel in Manchester framed upon the walls are selected verses of W.H. Auden's poem 'Night Mail', which was the famous centrepiece of the eponymous film. Auden's poem is the source, inspiration and character of 'Night Mails', a poem performed at a recent Association of Directors of Children's Services conference.

'Lock and Quay'

This Landmark Poem was embedded in the Surrey Quays development in 2016.

'Listening Post'

'Listening Post' was commissioned and read in Manchester on the anniversary of the Battle of the Somme in June 2016.

'Fallen'

'Fallen' was commissioned in 2016 by Coram and the Foundling Museum for the exhibition *Fallen Women*.

'Rest'

On 1 May 2009 Carol Ann Duffy became poet laureate. To mark the occasion BBC *Newsnight* asked a range of poets to give the new laureate some advice in verse form.

'Adventure Flight'

'Adventure Flight' was written for the FA Cup final in 2015. It was played online, on television and at Wembley on the day before the players came out onto the pitch.

Index of Titles

Index of First Lines